D1499183

John Locke and
Agrarian Capitalism

John Locke and Agrarian Capitalism

Neal Wood

University of California Press

Berkeley · Los Angeles · London

University of California Press
Berkeley and Los Angeles, California

University of California Press, Ltd.
London, England

Library of Congress Cataloging in Publication Data

Wood, Neal.
John Locke and agrarian capitalism.

Includes bibliographical references and index.
1. Locke, John, 1632–1704—Political science.
2. Great Britain—Economic conditions—17th century.
3. Capitalism—History—17th century. I. Title.
JC153.L87W66   1984   320'.01   83-24102
ISBN   0-520-05046-0

Printed in the United States of America

1 2 3 4 5 6 7 8 9

To the Memory
of My Parents
and My Brothers

Contents

Preface

This study, begun in the spring of 1981 and completed two years later, has indirectly resulted from a larger project on the social and political thought of John Locke. A Guggenheim Fellowship in 1971–72, a Leave Fellowship from The Canada Council in 1975–76, and a minor research grant and leaves of absence from York University made it possible for me to write "The Baconian Character of Locke's *Essay,*" *Studies in History and Philosophy of Science,* 6 (1975), pp. 43–84; and eventually after several interruptions, *The Politics of Locke's Philosophy: A Social Study of "An Essay Concerning Human Understanding"* (Berkeley, Los Angeles, London: University of California Press, 1983). Again I wish to express my debt to these institutions for their unstinting support, which enabled me to lay the groundwork for a second book on the greatest of English philosophers.

Some of the ideas presented here have in part been dealt with elsewhere: in a paper, "Baconian Natural History in Locke's Social Thought," read October 9, 1982, at the annual meeting in Rutgers University of the Northeast American Society for Eighteenth-Century Studies; and in an essay, "Baconian Natural History and Agrarian Capitalism in Locke's Social Thought," to appear in a forthcoming volume, *John Locke and the Political Thought of the 1680s,* edited by Gordon J. Schochet.

As usual my debt to Ellen Meiksins Wood is so enormous that even the most extravagant thanks cannot begin to suggest the value of her incisive criticism of every draft and her steadfast encouragement. My interest in agrarian capitalism was initially aroused by the brilliant articles of Robert Brenner, whose comments on two initial drafts and discussion of broader historical matters, and general enthusiasm, proved most useful and stimulating. After I had read her excellent book, Ann Kussmaul kindly shed further light on seventeenth-century English agricultural labor and saved me from a number of basic errors. Louis Lefeber was good enough to take time from his busy schedule and give me the benefit of his knowledge of early modern economic history and theory and his practical wisdom. David McNally allowed me to read in typescript portions of his important study of agrarian capitalism and the early development of the science of political economy, and over the years he has never hesitated to share with me his perceptive ideas on this and related matters. I am afraid that I may have unconsciously appropriated without due acknowledgement some of the Lockeian insights of Gordon Schochet who, as one might expect of a genuine liberal and specialist on toleration, has put up with my idiosyncrasies, backing me at every turn. Joyce Mastboom provided me with the basis of comparing the Dutch agrarian experience with that of early modern England, as well as supplying several helpful references; and Lorna Weir enlightened me on the subject of political arithmetic and corrected a few of my mistaken views. I can only express my appreciation to each and all of them with, of course, the conventional reminder that they are in no way responsible for what I have done with their aid and advice.

Thanks are also due to Marion Kozak for insisting that I read John Evelyn's *Sylva*, which proved to be far more relevant than I anticipated, and for generously allowing me to use her own copy. For the irksome task of checking citations, tracing down sources, and performing countless other bibliographic chores, I am most grateful to Peter Bowen, Lisa Price, and Gordon Sova. Sharon Edwards of Tunstall, Suffolk, typed the first draft promptly and expertly; and Ruth Griffin, of Glendon College, York University, and the secretarial staff of the Department of Political Science, York University, met my typing demands cheerfully and efficiently. Finally, I owe much to Mrs. Florence Knight of Toronto, who with customary spirit, accuracy, and dedication to her craft typed the final draft.

As the youngest and only surviving member of a family of authors who lovingly encouraged and nourished my early intellectual bent, I have dedicated the book to them.

Neal Wood
Toronto
September 10, 1983

Principal Primary Sources
and Abbreviations

Austen, Ralph	*Fruit Trees*	*A Treatise of Fruit-Trees* (Oxford, 1653).
	Spirituall Use	*The Spirituall Use of an Orchard; or Garden of Fruit-Trees,* in *Fruit-Trees,* cited above.
Blith, Walter	*English Improver*	*The English Improver, or a New Survey of Husbandry* (London, 1649).
	English Improver Improved	*The English Improver Improved or the Survey of Husbandry Surveyed* (London, 1653).
Boyle, Robert	*Usefulnesse*	*Some Considerations Touching the Usefulnesse of Experimental Naturall Philosophy. Propos'd in a Familiar Discourse to a Friend, by Way of Invitation to the Study of It* (2nd ed.; Oxford, 1664–1671), vol. 1.
Child, Robert	*Large Letter*	*A Large Letter Concerning the Defects and Remedies of English Husbandry, Written to Mr. Samuel Hartlib,* in Hartlib, *Legacie,* cited below.

Dymock, Cressy	*New Divisions*	*A Discovery for New Divisions, or, Setting out of Lands, as to the Best Forme: Imparted in a Letter to Samuel Hartlib, Esquire,* in Hartlib, *Discoverie,* cited below.
Evelyn, John	*Kalendarium*	*Kalendarium hortanse* (3rd ed.; London, 1669), in Evelyn, *Sylva,* cited below.
	Pomona	*Pomona* (London, 1670), in Evelyn, *Sylva,* cited below.
	Sylva	*Sylva or a Discourse of Forest-Trees and the Propagation of Timber in His Majesties Dominions* (2nd ed.; London, 1670).
	Terra	*The Terra: A philosophical discourse of Earth,* in *Silva* . . . (3rd ed.; York, 1801), vol. 2.
Hartlib, Samuel	*Discoverie*	*A Discoverie for Division or Setting out of Land, as to the Best Form* (London, 1653).
	Legacie	*Samuel Hartlib His Legacie: Or an Enlargement of A Discourse of Husbandry Used in Brabant and Flaunders* (London, 1652).
Houghton, John	*Letters*	*A Collection of Letters for the Improvement of Husbandry and Trade* (London, 1681–83), 2 vols.
Locke, John	*Conduct*	*Of the Conduct of the Understanding,* ed. Francis W. Garforth (New York: Teachers College Press, 1966).

Correspondence

The Correspondence of John Locke, ed. E. S. de Beer (Oxford: Clarendon Press, 1976–), 8 vols.; 7 vols. to date.

Education

Some Thoughts Concerning Education, in *The Educational Writings of John Locke*, ed. James L. Axtell (Cambridge: Cambridge University Press, 1968).

Essay

An Essay Concerning Human Understanding, 4th ed. (1700), ed. Peter H. Nidditch (Oxford: Clarendon Press, 1975).

Essay Concerning Toleration

"An Essay Concerning Toleration," in H. R. Fox Bourne, *The Life of John Locke* (London: King, 1876), vol. 1, pp. 174–94.

First Tract

The First Tract on Government, in *Two Tracts on Government*, ed. and trans. Philip Abrams (Cambridge: Cambridge University Press, 1967).

First Treatise

Two Treatises of Government: A Critical Edition with an Introduction and Apparatus Criticus, ed. Peter Laslett (2nd ed.; Cambridge: Cambridge University Press, 1970).

Law of Nature

Essays on the Law of Nature, ed. and trans. W. von Leyden (2nd impression; Oxford: Clarendon Press, 1958).

Poor Laws

"Proposal for Reform of the

Poor Laws," in H. R. Fox Bourne, *The Life of John Locke* (London: King, 1876), vol. 2, pp. 377–91.

Reasonableness   *The Reasonableness of Christianity, as Delivered in the Scriptures,* in *Works,* cited below, vol. 6.

Second Treatise   Laslett edition cited above for *First Treatise.*

1668   *Some of the Consequences That Are Like to Follow upon Lessening of Interest to 4 Percent,* in William Letwin, *The Origins of Scientific Economics: English Economic Thought, 1660–1776* (London: Methuen, 1963), pp. 273–300.

1692   *Some Considerations of the Consequences of the Lowering of Interest, and Raising the Value of Money. In a Letter Sent to a Member of Parliament, 1691,* in *Works,* cited below, vol. 4.

Toleration   *A Letter on Toleration,* in *Epistola de Tolerantia: A Letter on Toleration,* ed. with preface by Raymond Klibansky, trans. with introduction and notes by J. W. Gough (Oxford: Clarendon Press, 1968).

Works   *The Works of John Locke* (9th ed.; London, 1794), 9 vols.

Mascall, Leonard   *New Art*   *The Country-Mans New Art of Planting and Graffing* (London, 1651).

Petty, Sir William	*Political Arithmetick*	*Political Arithmetick* (London, 1690).
	Treatise	*A Treatise of Taxes and Contributions* (2nd ed.; London, 1667).
Reeve, Gabriel	*Directions*	*Directions Left by a Gentleman to His Sonnes for the Improvement of Barren and Heathy Land* (London, 1670).
Smith, Sir Thomas	*Republica*	*De republica anglorum*, ed. Mary Dewar (Cambridge: Cambridge University Press, 1982), originally written in the early 1560s and first published in 1583.
Weston, Sir Richard	*Discours*	*A Discours of Husbandrie Used in Brabant and Flaunders, Shewing Wonderful Improvement of Land There* (1645), in Reeve, *Directions*, cited above.

CHAPTER ONE

A Question of Method

At the risk of considerable oversimplification, two "pure" forms of studying past political thought can be identified: the *philosophical* and the *historical*.[1] In practice, scholarly efforts lie somewhere between the two ideal types, most being closer to the philosophical than to the historical pole. The philosophical mode concentrates on the internal relationships of the words, propositions, and ideas of a classic text of political theory. Emphasis is given to the analysis and assessment of concepts, the logic of argumentation, and the consistency of the major political ideas, often with the aim of evaluating the thinker's contribution to one of the so-called perennial problems of political philosophy such as obligation, authority, or justice. Although the notions thus scrutinized tend to be treated as constituting an autonomous world of abstractions without any external referents, history is frequently employed to "illuminate" a text by way of "background" and to "enrich" our understanding of it. History is also used in the form of constructing a genealogy of ideas, tracing the influence of a thinker's predecessors and contemporaries on his own thought in the way that typifies the "history of ideas" genre. Despite the resistance to historicizing a text, however, even the most extreme philosophical analyst cannot altogether dispense with history. Only by reference to and reliance on history can a correct chronological sequence of texts and thinkers be assured; the places, names, events, and institutions mentioned in the text be known; and the language of the author be grasped. Some understanding of the circumstances under which the text was written is also usually recognized as necessary to an internal philosophical examination. Apart from these functions, history has little role in the philosophical mode.

In comparison, the historical approach rests on the assumption that the meaning of a classic text can be established only if it is firmly situated in the appropriate social, political, and economic context and the relationship between the theorists' realm of ideas and the world of action in which they lived and wrote is carefully defined. The logic of ideas must always be securely tied to the logic of practice, to the everyday life of the age, to the turmoil of the political forum and the hustle and bustle of the market. Far from neglecting the internal assessment of the text, the historical mode requires that each step of the analysis be informed by what can be discovered about the concrete human activity of the time. Because ideas and actions are mutually dependent and interpenetrating, forming a seamless web, history should never serve as mere background to a political theory in a static and lifeless way. Theorist and theory are essential and integral components of the historical process. To separate the two is to obscure and distort the nature of history, human creativity, and the ideas of the theorist.

From the historical standpoint, a text in the history of political thought is a valuable social document. When properly studied, it may reveal something of significance about the institutions, arrangements, values, beliefs, and attitudes of its times, just as do other documents at the disposal of the historian: diaries, journals, commonplace books, letters, poems, plays, broadsheets, tracts, technical manuals, and state papers. Because the central focus of a text in political theory is on the nature of the state, entailing prescriptions by the author for its conservation, reform, or radical reconstruction, we have for our use a convenient means of access to the historical reality of the period.

This does not mean that a text accurately mirrors its age, or necessarily embodies the spirit of a people, or satisfactorily encapsulates their historical experience. The image of the past may be and usually is variously distorted, as in most documents examined by the historian. One such skewed vision of the historical scene is so commonplace as to be barely worth mentioning except for the fact that students of past political thought rarely give it the attention it warrants. Prior to the French Revolution and the advent of industrial capitalism, the classic texts in political theory, with some notable exceptions, are "histories from above," essentially reflections on the existing state and the need for its preservation or change written from the perspective of a member or client of the ruling classes. These ascendant social groupings were normally a tiny minority of leisured, literate, nonlaboring dignitaries of landed wealth who dominated a vast majority of propertyless, uncultured, manual laborers whose sweat and toil maintained the institutionalized system of power, hierarchy, and authority we call the state. The history of precapitalist political thought, in fact, can be said to have as one of its major themes the problem of "lord versus peasant," more often than not from the standpoint of the lord. Throughout the precapitalist world, numerous peasants—living at a bare subsistence level and politically powerless—fed, clothed, and housed the lordly minority; manned the armed forces; and through their surplus labor extracted by payment of rents, fees, tributes, and taxes enabled their superiors to live in security, comfort, and ease. The fundamental problem addressed by most precapitalist political theorists, although customarily framed less clearly and unambiguously, was how to preserve and strengthen this or a similar exploitative and repressive hierarchical system of power. On the one hand, a united front must be secured among the lords; on the other hand, the peasants must be controlled and rendered into a manageable and reliable work force. The precapitalist political thinkers, however, were not concerned solely with prescribing such social and governmental arrangements but also with offering a theoretical justification for them, with providing the division between rulers and ruled with an aura of authority and legitimacy based on complex arguments derived variously from human nature, metaphysics, religion, theology, history, and so on. In order to recognize these preoccupations, one need only keep in mind the works of Plato, Aristotle, Polybius, Cicero, St. Augustine, John of Salisbury, St. Thomas, Marsiglio of Padua, William of Ockham, and Bodin.

The full character of this "history from above" is only made clear by relating it to what can be learned about the "history from below" of the times of the specific thinkers.[2] The meaning of the classic text in any but the most simplistic sense, consequently, cannot be understood without locating it in the historical totality of which it is a part. Thus, by placing text in context, joining history from above with history from below, the ideas of the author will be perceived in connection with their material conditions. This is the basic objective of an authentic social history of political thought. It should seek to embed the ideas of the theorists in the social matrix, to associate their views with what was occurring in the social universe. The question to be asked, if the meaning of their theories is to be ascertained, is how their ideas relate to the structure of their society, the nature of its government and law, the crucial political conflicts, and the system of class and status. What, if any, is the relevance of productive forces, the relations of production, the division of labor, and the mode of surplus extraction to an understanding of their views? How does each of these factors in relation to the others help to elucidate their realm of political ideas as an interconnected whole? How is this totality of ideas and actions, in turn, related to what went on before in the society and what was to occur in the future? This kind of analysis may rescue the history of political thought from stale antiquarianism and sterile abstractionism by restoring the text to where it was conceived and belongs, to the historical process, one of constant flux and change as well as of stability and continuity. When so approached, the text is reinstated as a dynamic and living element of history, a meaningful and vital constituent of the ebb and flow of civilized life.

The danger lies not so much in historicizing a text in this fashion as in over-philosophizing it. For too many scholars, past political ideas seem to constitute a sphere of abstractions with their own life and logic, almost completely cut off from the greater historical world of which they are significant components. If past political theory were strictly speaking a matter of philosophy alone, this attitude might possibly be legitimate; but some exceedingly important and influential political theorists—Polybius, Marsiglio, Machiavelli, Bodin, Winstanley, Harrington, Rousseau, Burke, Madison—could in no technical sense be called philosophers.

More significantly, political theory, whether the creation of a philosopher or nonphilosopher, is fundamentally political, and the political is never simply a matter of intellectual or linguistic manipulation. Language is obviously a major factor in politics, but words are a means of mobilizing and articulating interests, of resolving disputes, and of creating authority. Language facilitates the communication of bread-and-butter issues, of matters of life and death. Political acts comprehend more than words. Words are always supplemented and even displaced by partially nonverbal actions: ceremony, ritual, conspicuous display, demonstrations, strikes, unemployment, starvation, imprisonment, execution, exile, assassination, revolution, and war. Conflict and competition, although expressed in words, are rooted in the material conditions of a society. The reduction of politics to linguistics and word games tends to trivialize a crucial human activity. Politics refers not only to mental and verbal activity but also "to" physical activity relevant to the public arena, to the state and the functioning of the state, and to the all-embracing structure of power in a given society.

Political theorists are political actors on the stage of history insofar as they wish through their theorizing to impel their readers to act politically by ultimately affecting the nature of the state, either by supporting or altering it. Their act of writing is a response to what they feel are social and political problems of the greatest urgency, an attempt to convince their limited audience of well-placed readers in turn to act as they persuade them to by the most intellectually cogent arguments at their command. The classic text, customarily written in times of social and political turmoil, was designed to be a weapon of ideas in the debate and struggle to define and promote the public interest or common good. To treat a text as if its ideas were isolated from the social and political conflict in which they participated is radically to depoliticize past political thought, and, more important, to dehumanize it. The removal of political theory from its historical scene, in short, devitalizes it in a very rudimentary sense. Political theorists were profoundly concerned with essential questions that involved human beings often in a contest for their livelihood and survival. Unless their theorizing is restored to the historical context out of which it came, much of its distinctively human character will be lost beyond recovery.

One reason why the philosophical mode may be more fashionable than the historical approach among historians of political thought has possibly less to do with intellectual conviction than with ingrained cultural attitude. Since Plato, the philosopher has been placed on a pedestal. Of all mental activities, philosophy has generally been considered the highest, and the material world, to which much of philosophy since Plato has traditionally opposed its sphere of pure ideas, has often been seen as a rather grubby, transient realm of necessity.

One of the traits of philosophy found in Plato and continuing to the present has been its role of mystification. Philosophers may sometimes indulge in such intellectual obscurantism as to disguise most effectively in the name of "truth" the real social and political implications of what they are saying—often of a distinctly partisan nature—from the unwary reader. Cicero furthered the view of Plato by popularizing the idea of the philosopher as a detached and impartial observer, far removed from mundane affairs and free from any taint of self-interest. Moreover, philosophy was always deemed to be a calling suitable for a gentleman. This syndrome of snobbery is still manifest in some academic and intellectual circles. Philosophers, it is sometimes felt, form a breed apart, intellectually more sophisticated and intelligent than lesser mortals, the peers of the academic realm whose pronouncements on a diversity of nonphilosophic subjects are received with deference. The frequently heard judgment of disdain that a subject is of "little philosophical interest" sometimes carries the patronizing implication that the matter is intellectually inferior and really not worthy of consideration by finer minds. Perhaps Marx's cardinal sin was not that he was a revolutionary but that he was a renegade philospher who turned to economics and history. Small wonder, then, that historians of political thought, many of whom are trained as political scientists and who constantly abstract political theories from the classic philosophic systems, should prefer to call their work "political philosophy." They are gentlemen and scholars and, within departments of politics, superior beings, if surrogate philosophers. Why should they defile the world of pure political ideas by dirtying their hands with the data of social and economic history? And those who deign to ground the history of political ideas in material conditions are dismissed as reductionists, in contrast to their own open-minded, dispassionate, and objective scholarship.

None of these comments is intended to denigrate or belittle the valuable contribution made by many of those who work within the philosophical mode.[3] They clearly dominate contemporary scholarship in the history of political thought. If, however, the history of political thought is to continue to thrive and advance, more attention in the future should be given to contextual analysis in the way just outlined. Otherwise, the discipline may very well degenerate into scholastic disputation of a narrowly technical kind, with little relevance to thought and action at the end of the twentieth century. Fruitful new areas of inquiry may be overlooked, and exciting possibilities of creative breakthroughs may be closed. Very little movement in the historical direction, unfortunately, can be detected. The few scholarly commentators pursuing the historical approach are in the main historians whose treatment of political theory and theorists is only incidental to more inclusive interests.[4]

Two widely acclaimed books have been heralded for restoring in different ways the study of past political thought to the historical domain: C. B. Macpherson's *The Political Theory of Possessive Individualism* and Quentin Skinner's *The Foundations of Modern Political Thought*.[5] Close scrutiny of them, however, reveals more philosophical orientation and less historical analysis than is commonly supposed. In view of this unconventional evaluation, each merits brief attention in light of the previous remarks.

Although Macpherson writes from a Marxist perspective, his study of seventeenth-century English political thought is surprisingly unhistorical. He is less concerned with historical processes and changing social structures than with employing heuristic models that he constructs with little detailed reference to concrete circumstances and developments. He begins with the fundamental assumption that seventeenth-century England was a market society, but nowhere does he demonstrate the historical validity of this contention, a decided defect given the doubts of many scholars on the subject. For all practical purposes a rigorous historical investigation of the nature of English production and productive relations has little part in his enterprise. A systematic historical analysis of class structure that would provide an informative context for the political ideas of Hobbes and Locke is singularly missing. What little is said about the historical reality of productive relations—for example, about the extent of wage labor—is itself open to considerable question.

The main point to be made about Macpherson's project, however, is that historical reality seems to be of little consequence to it. His argument does not seem to depend on whether or not the England of Hobbes and Locke was actually a market society. Instead, he seems primarily interested in showing that their theories are based on assumptions that conform to his own abstractly constructed model of "market society." Far from being historical, the intellectual style of

Macpherson's argument belongs to the tradition of philosophical analysis. He characteristically attempts to show how a political theory, from premises to conclusion, can be rendered consistent only if the theorist's assumptions are identified, in the cases of Hobbes and Locke, for example, their assumption of a market society. History intervenes, when necessary, only as a link in the theorist's chain of argumentation, as an explicit or implicit theoretical assumption. So, for instance, the theoretical assumptions of a (theoretically constructed) "market society"—not its historical reality—are for Macpherson a necessary although hidden link in Hobbes's argument for a sovereign power. Without such a link, according to Macpherson, Hobbes's argument would be logically inconsistent or incomplete.

For Macpherson, any criticism of his textual interpretation that refers to its historical weakness would be beside the point. He most likely would be unmoved even by the suggestion that his model of market society is so abstract and broadly delineated that it might apply, for instance, almost as well to the late Roman Republic as it does to seventeenth-century England. To Macpherson, the most telling attack on his interpretation would probably be one that demonstrated a *logical*, not an historical, inconsistency between the assumptions built into the market model and the conclusion that he says it necessarily entails. So, by way of illustration, if one could show that the necessity of a sovereign power does not logically follow from the assumption of a market society, or that such a necessity could equally well derive from a wholly different set of assumptions, Macpherson might very well feel inclined to reconsider his interpretation of Hobbes. It is precisely here that the weakness of Macpherson's approach becomes most visible. The absence of any historical check on his philosophic argument, of any consideration of historical plausibility, accounts for many of the difficulties in his interpretation of classic thinkers like Hobbes and Locke. Indeed, his basic argument tends to be circular, for the initial premise of a market society seems to be derived from those very traits of the political thought of Hobbes and Locke that he proposes to identify, namely characteristics of a market mentality, "possessive individualism."

The major flaw in Macpherson's overly abstract and unhistorical procedure is perhaps best illuminated, as suggested above, by his mistreatment of the question of Hobbes and the concept of sovereignty. Instead of trying to locate Hobbes's political theory in the context of historical processes actually occurring in seventeenth-century England, or in Europe generally, Macpherson attempts to reconstruct the hidden assumptions logically entailed by Hobbes's argument, and he concludes that his belief in the need for a supreme sovereign power proceeds from implicit presuppositions that obtain only in a "market society." This conclusion is drawn with little reference to the historical circumstances in which a sovereign power actually did become necessary and possible in Europe. Aside from questioning Macpherson's interpretation of Hobbes's notions of man and of seventeenth-century English society as essentially bourgeois, we have to ask what was actually occurring in England that may have led Hobbes to develop a theory of sovereignty. For we know that in the previous century Bodin had postulated a conception of sovereignty similar to Hobbes's, and few would claim that Bodin's notion of man was bourgeois or that his society was bourgeois. Whether the two ideas of sovereignty were in response to comparable practical circumstances can only be determined by an empirical investigation that might at the same time be the initial step in placing Hobbes's political thought in its historical context, thus avoiding the pitfalls of Macpherson's mode of analysis. In designing his own concept of sovereignty Bodin seemed to be centrally concerned not with a market society but about the quasi-feudal fragmentation of political power and jurisdiction and the "baronial" conflict that prevailed in France, and the efforts of the "absolute" monarchy to overcome this parcelization of the state. In other words, an historical analysis might lead one to question whether the belief in the need for a sovereign power logically entails the assumption of a "market society."

Had Macpherson relied more on the historical mode and less on conceptual analysis, a market-oriented approach to political economy, and a Weberian "ideal-type" methodology, a number of these confusions and omissions might not have marred his account of seventeenth-century English political thought, and it might have been brought closer to the social reality of the age. There are many excellent things in his analysis, but he is just as wrong in his contention that English society was bourgeois as he is that Hobbes was a bourgeois philosopher.[6] The interpretation of Locke is somewhat closer to the mark, as we shall see, but not for the reasons given by Macpherson.

Professor Skinner's brilliant examination of a host of major and minor thinkers in the seminal 300 years from 1300 to 1600 is informed by a methodology worked out in a number of philosophically sophisticated essays written previously.[7] In brief outline his position is that the meaning of a classic text can be recaptured by locating it in the appropriate ideological context—the shared vocabulary, conventions, and assumptions of one of several realms of common discourse of an age, for example: scholasticism, humanism, Lutheranism, Calvinism. "Meaning" is restricted by Skinner to the technical linguistic sense, to refer to common usage. Once the text has been associated with a specific "paradigm," that paradigm is carefully reconstructed by studying the many minor authors who have been responsible for its development.[8] The classic text is then compared to the paradigm in order to show how the language of the author conforms to or departs from it. The more original the thinker, the greater will be his deviation from the paradigm. The original thinker, in effect, uses much of the language of the paradigm, to give it new meaning: it is a question of new wine in old bottles, with the result that the paradigm is revolutionized. By following such a procedure the historian of political thought properly attempts to recover the full meaning of a text instead of analyzing it from the standpoint of his own values and assumptions or in terms of its contribution to one of the great perennial problems of philosophical discourse.

Students of past political thought are certainly indebted to Skinner for his basic perception of the importance of situating the classic texts in their ideological paradigms. What he has done in an impressive way is to give to the traditional history of ideas a "lateral" and "collective" dimension as well as a "linear" and "individual" one. His emphasis on the historicity of the text and his rejection of the "perennial problems" approach can only be of distinct aid in making the history of political thought an authentic historical study.

The most serious shortcoming of Skinner's approach, despite his emphasis on contextual analysis and the historicity of the text, paradoxical as it may seem in view of what has been said, is its unhistorical character. It is somewhat ironic that Skinner, who is a trained historian and experienced teacher of history, should display so little feeling for history, beyond the history of ideas. "Historical context," as he employs the expression, signifies primarily the ideological paradigm. History for him is fundamentally the history of ideas, and although his work is an indisputable advance over what often has been previously accomplished within that genre, it still remains largely concerned with the relationships that exist among linguistic formulations. Indeed, he tends to see language as central to politics; politics is a kind of language game. Politics basically involves the manipulation and maneuver of linguistic signs, the tactics and strategy of their employment. Politics is largely concerned with ideas in abstraction, more or less isolated from their material contexts. From this standpoint Skinner's position appears to be on the philosophical side of political history. His mode of historical inquiry would seem to rest on idealist assumptions.

Nowhere are these observations more clearly demonstrated than in his actual handling of the second stage of his investigative procedure. Skillful and perceptive as his ideological analysis often is, the treatment of the social and political contexts of the texts and ideologies tends to be far less acute, even verging on the pedestrian background approach typical of so much of the history of political ideas. He never tries to identify in a systematic fashion the vital connection between the historical context of ideology and the historical context of society, polity, and economy. His contextual realm of common discourse is basically a sphere of interrelated and disembodied ideas with apparently little relationship to the material life of man. What is actually said about social and political arrangements suggests a noticeable absence of a dynamic process of basic change from his notion of history. The examination in *The Foundations* of three of the most important centuries of European history as a prelude to modernity fails to discuss in detail agriculture, the aristocracy and peasantry, land distribution and tenure, the social division of labor, social protest and conflict, population, urbanization, trade, commerce, manufacture, and the burgher class. The relationship between the critical changes occurring in these vital sectors and the social and political ideas is never adequately treated. This kind of neglect is all the more puzzling in view of the fact that one of his central themes is the intellectual and material preconditions giving rise to the modern conception of the state.[9] The "material preconditions" discussed include none of the far-reaching social developments that so indelibly stamped European history; they are almost exclusively of a formal political and governmental nature, as are the contexts he gives for the ideologies. The link between the major social forces and economic developments occurring over the full time-span of the three centuries and the govenments and politics of specific states at particular times is never really investigated.

When ideas are related to practical politics and government, it is often in an "episodic" manner, as in Skinner's treatment of the Florentine context of Machiavelli's thought or of Hobbes and the Engagement Controversy.[10] The full sweep of history, the interconnection of ideas with long-term social, political, and economic forces and trends is seldom considered. We are exposed, instead, to the atomization of history, its break-up into discrete, self-contained segments, with very little explanation of their relationship to what went on before or what was to follow. For heuristic reasons, it is necessary to sever the seamless web of history, but Skinner fails to convey to his reader how the segment, thus isolated and evaluated, results from past circumstances and helps change the future. A certain similarity exists on this score between his treatment of history and that of the new revisionist historians of seventeenth-century England like Conrad Russell.[11] The historian, or so the revisionists maintain, should subject a particular event or complex of events to microscopic examination without the intrusion into the analysis of how those events fit into the continuing historical process. Whatever its merits in the analysis of isolated historical events, this procedure is especially problematic in a study that purports to examine longterm developments. For Skinner the intimate relationships between an evolving social structure and existing political circumstances, and in turn between them and economic factors long in the making, seem to have little bearing on the form of the political ideas. As a consequence much of the historical meaning of the text is lost.

What follows, therefore, is a modest attempt to remedy several of the deficiencies of the philosophical approach by suggesting how the historical mode of analysis can be used in the study of some of the principal social and political ideas of John Locke. An effort will be made to situate a number of his ideas in a common realm of discourse, one, however, quite different from that of natural law, which for James Tully is basic to a full understanding of Locke's *Second Treatise*.[12] The realm of discourse selected here for examination, as will become clear, is related not only to the social realities of late Stuart England but also to the historical process shaping our own world. The result perhaps will be a perception of Locke in a new light.

Locke will be identified as a "theorist" of early agrarian capitalism, not as a thinker who articulated the interests and aspirations of an incipient mercantile and manufacturing bourgeoisie. The evidence for this radical thesis—in addition to Locke's interest in agriculture and in the quality of the gentry—depends on an examination of his economic thought between 1668 and 1692 and of selected ideas of chapter 5, "Of Property," of the *Second Treatise*. In 1668 he wrote a memorandum on the question of the interest rate and in 1692, still retaining his original views, published an expanded version of it, a major technical treatise in the history of economic thought, *Some Considerations of the Consequences of the Lowering of Interest and Raising the Value of Money*. The economic ideas of the two works, it will be argued, formed an overarching context, essentially stable and unchanging, within which chapter 5, most probably drafted between 1679 and 1681, should be properly assessed if its historical significance is to be understood. Together, the three works reflect basic structural changes in the social relations of production then occurring in the English countryside, specifically those related to the development of the agrarian capitalism that was coming to dominate the corn and mixed corn and livestock areas of the south and east. Each work exhibits a fundamental concern with the agrarian sector and with agricultural productivity. The basic historical significance of Locke's ideas in the three writings is reflected by their break with the time-hallowed attitude toward farming and landed property and by their relevance to what we know of the subsequent agrarian transformation of the eighteenth century and the accompanying creation of the science of political economy, instrumental in shaping the material and ideological matrix out of which classic British industrial capitalism of the nineteenth century emerged.

Both the memorandum of 1668 and chapter 5 apply the mode of Baconian natural history to the analysis of social problems, although in different ways. Unlike the two economic works, however, chapter 5 employs the conceptual language of the Baconian agricultural improvers and reformers in the latter half of the seventeenth century and addresses some of the same agrarian questions that they did. Their tracts were known to Locke, and their views, which were part of the common currency of the day among the more enlightened country gentlemen, seem to have had a profound influence on the form taken by many of the central ideas and their interrelationships in the chapter. Contrary to the argument of James Tully, who in his recent application of the Skinnerian mode of analysis finds the key to the meaning of chapter 5 in Locke's use of the normative vocabulary of the common natural law discourse of the period, my analysis concludes that only by reference to the constant of the economic ideas between 1668 and 1692 and to the realm of the Baconian improvers' discourse—both intimately related to the basic changes in the material conditions of late Stuart England—can the chapter be adequately assessed and appreciated. Some of Locke's subsequent thoughts on apparently unrelated subjects, moreover, such as in *An Essay Concerning Human Understanding* (1690) and *Some Thoughts Concerning Education* (1693), seem to be congruent and in harmony with this conclusion. Indeed, it may be ventured that the thesis that Locke was a theorist of early agrarian capitalism, once fully explained and with its implications clearly understood, provides a unifying element in the diversity of his thought. Perhaps such an approach will help to rescue Locke's social and political ideas from the world of abstractions and relocate them where they originated, in the practical problems of English everyday life in the seventeenth century.

CHAPTER TWO

Locke's Interest
in Husbandry

The widely held view of Locke as bourgeois philosopher and ideologist of early capitalism has been largely due to the scholarship of C. B. Macpherson and Leo Strauss.[1] Over the last twenty years, however, Professor Macpherson's interpretation in particular has been placed under the critical microscope, resulting in its rejection by a number of specialists. Leading the attack in 1960, Peter Laslett began by admitting that Locke was born into the "classical atmosphere of early capitalism" and by acknowledging his Puritan background, lifelong investment in commercial enterprise, and unrelenting enmity toward the idle poor.[2] Then Laslett pointed out that Locke "profoundly mistrusted commerce and commercial men," suspected the motives of the founders of the Bank of England, and "despised" the emerging medical and legal professions. Laslett concluded: "No simple conception of 'ideology' will relate Locke's thought with social dynamics." He can only be described "as an independent, free-moving intellectual, aware as others were not of the direction of social change." At the end of the decade, John Dunn expressed agreement with Laslett's verdict by asserting that Locke "at no point in his works devotes extended moral enthusiasm to the role of the merchant or industrial producer," and he took issue with Macpherson on a number of important matters.[3] More recently, several broadsides have been directed against the "bourgeois thesis." Keith Tribe judged that "it is not only wage-labour which is absent from Locke's writings; the capitalist finds no space there either."[4] The opinion was seconded by James Tully: "The capitalist not only

15

never appears in the *Two Treatises*; there is no place for him to appear."[5]

Something can be said for both sides of the argument. The "pro-bourgeois" camp is quite right in finding historically new and distinctive elements in Locke's approach, and the "anti-bourgeois" critics are equally correct in stressing Locke's antipathy to merchants, monied men, and commerce. The defenders of the bourgeois position err in thinking that Locke's England was a developed market society in which economic behavior was most commonly motivated by "economic," in the sense of market, considerations. These assumptions render them all too easy prey for their opponents, as does the view that to be a capitalist philosopher required Locke to justify the activities of the fledgling mercantile and manufacturing bourgeoisie. The critics, on the other hand, never precisely define capitalism and the bourgeoisie, nor do they seem to recognize that classic capitalism of the nineteenth century was the result of a lengthy and complex historical process. No one can deny the roots of capitalism in English society of the seventeenth century, if not before, but to state this is not to argue that the bare beginnings are identical with what eventuated at a much later date, or that at such an early stage infant mercantile and manufacturing capitalism should be the sole focus of attention.

Instead, perhaps, a search should be made for indications of basic changes occurring in the social relations of production, which on a large scale were radically to alter productive forces in the future, in order to determine how, if at all, Locke's thought expressed or illuminated these incipient changes. Because England was predominantly an agricultural nation where wealth, social prestige, and political power depended so fundamentally on landed property, one might obviously look first to the countryside for evidence of changes in the social relations of production that were later to become essential to a fully developed capitalism.

Curiously, no attempt has been made in the debate about Locke to relate his social and political thought to the emergence of agrarian capitalism in sixteenth and seventeenth-century England, a development that was unique in Europe.[6] From the late middle ages to Locke's day the system of property relations in the English countryside had been undergoing a profound change. Lords and gentry had gradually been extending their control over cultivable land. By the sixteenth century direct agricultural production was primarily in the hands of their free tenants, the former villeins, who since the end of serfdom had over the years become copyholders subject to the arbitrary fines of gentlemanly landlords. With the exception of a few ancient freeholders, most of the celebrated yeomanry of the sixteenth century consisted of these tenants, who were freeholders in their own right but who depended to a marked degree on income from their copyholds and other kinds of leaseholds. Sir Thomas Smith, in an all but forgotten definition of the sixteenth-century yeoman, makes much of this clear and more:

I call him a yeoman whom our lawes doe call *Legalem hominem*, a worde familiar to writtes and enquestes, which is a freeman borne English, who may dispend of his owne free lande in yerely revenue to the summe of xl.s. sterling by the yeare. . . . This sort of people confesse themselves to be no gentlemen, but give honour to al which be or take upon them to be gentlemen, and yet they have a certaine preheminence and more estimation than laborers and artificers, and commonly live welthilie, keepe good houses, do their businesse, and travaile to get riches: these be (for the most part) fermors to gentlemen, and with grasing, frequenting of markettes, and keeping servauntes, not idle servants as the gentleman doth, but such as get both their owne living and parte of their maisters: by these meanes doe come to such wealth, that they are able and daily doe buy the landes of unthriftie gentlemen.[7]

As "fermors to gentlemen," then, sixteenth-century yeomen were tenants who leased land for cultivation.[8]

With the rapid population increase since the end of the fifteenth century accompanied by spiraling prices, inflated interest rates, and the growing need of the burgeoning number of gentlemanly landlords for ever greater cash incomes from rents, yeomen leaseholders were forced into a fierce competitive struggle to produce for the market. In order to maintain and increase high rents landlord also vied with landlord for choice tenants, and they found it in their interest to cooperate with tenants in bearing the cost of capital improvements and in other matters of mutual concern. The intense contest for survival among the yeomen tenants—requiring the acquisition of sufficient funds for the payment of soaring rents, exorbitant rates of interest, and the purchase of necessary goods and services—forced them to increase the productivity of their holdings, to expand them, and to cut costs. A yeoman, if he were not to go under, had to learn to specialize and invest his profits in new leases and improvement. Through care, industry, thrift, and enterprising shrewdness, these strategies increased his competitiveness in the market and his chances of survival, and in the process the small, less daring and innovative holder was squeezed out. Apart from striving to attract and hold promising tenants, landlords with serious commercial intentions for their home farms were caught up in the same market-induced competition with the yeomen, and as time passed some sought even greater profits by becoming leaseholders themselves.

In response to the needs of these capitalist farmers, far-reaching changes were slowly transforming rural England. Productivity was being raised and cultivation extended by crucial agricultural techniques such as convertible husbandry, floating water meadows, the use of new fallow crops and selected grasses, the drainage of fens and marshlands, manuring, and the development of stock breeding. Fundamental to these alterations were the reorganization of farms and the emergence of a new farming mentality. Estates were enlarged by engrossment and enclosure. Traditional family subsistence farms, at least in the south and east, were slowly replaced by efficiently operated agrarian enterprises producing for the market, utilizing wage labor, and reinvesting profits in the expansion of production. The following description of the Berkshire yeoman Robert Loder, in the second decade of the seventeenth century, typifies the rise of the capitalist farmer:

He was not content with subsistence farming, but grew for commercial marketing the wheat and barley which he knew would sell readily at London and at the market towns within reach of his estate. He improved his land in the manner advocated by the plethora of books on good husbandry which appeared in Elizabethan and early Stuart times and bought lime, for example, every year to fertilize his ground. As the editor of his accounts has written of him: "He wanted as large a financial return for his expenditure of capital and managerial work as he could get, and did his utmost to maintain it." It is hard to believe that Loder's approach was not typical of hundreds more, for whenever an individual farmer's records have survived, their predominant themes are experimentation and diversity of farming.[9]

These changes were accompanied by growth of a rural wage-labor force and its increasing specialization, by the division between land-owning and farming, and by the appearance of middlemen in the various stages of production prior to marketing. From mid-seventeenth century the number of peasant freeholders sharply declined, the victims of the drop in grain prices and the pressure of large proprietors. Land ownership was becoming concentrated in the hands of an ever smaller number of landlords. Agrarian organization of the countryside began to manifest the triadic nature—so familiar in the writings of the classical political economists—of landlord, capitalist tenant farmer, and laborer, each respectively living on rents, profits, and wages. Agrarian capitalism in Locke's day probably dominated the corn and livestock areas in the southern downlands (Chalk, Southdown, Northdown, Chiltern, Northwold, Oxford Heights "countries") and in the east (Norfolk Heathlands, East Norfolk, Breckland, Sandling's countries).[10] In fact, it might not be rash to say that by Locke's death the majority of English capitalists with the greatest total assets consisted not of merchants, financiers, and manufacturers, but of farmers.

Because Locke's lifetime was a watershed between traditional and capitalist agriculture, at least in the English arable, his writings could be expected to offer some sign of these far-reaching changes. It will, therefore, be useful to define as carefully as possible his association with agriculture. We may thus begin to see Locke in a new light, as a "theorist" of early agrarian capitalism.[11]

A word about the use of the terms *bourgeois* and *capitalist* may at this point prove helpful. Since the nineteenth century the words have often been employed interchangeably. In the broad sense, the "bourgeoisie," particularly in Marxist literature, have come to mean members of the ruling classes in the capitalist state, businessmen engaged in capitalist enterprise, and administrators and professionals—together often called the "middle classes." Traditionally, however, to simplify a complicated question of usage, a "bourgeois" was a burgher, a city or town-dweller who earned a livelihood by being a merchant, master craftsman, manufacturer, banker, speculator, rentier, "professional," man of letters, or official, depending for his income on profits, interest, rents, salaries, stipends, royalties, and commissions. He was distinguished from the landed upper classes by birth, status, activity, manners, and a way of life perhaps more sombre and less ostentatious than that of the rural elite. The capitalist either owns or controls the use of the means of production that is manned by wage laborers, free direct producers who in the historical process have lost control of the means of production and whose labor power has become a commodity to be sold to the capitalist in the market. The capitalist lives on profits derived from the expropriation of the surplus value produced by the workers. His economic behavior is motivated by a desire to maximize profit and minimize loss, and the necessity to accumulate and expand capital. He is willing to bear short-term losses for long-term gains and displays a rational, calculating attitude toward his business, profit from which is constantly reinvested in order to expand production, reduce costs, and thus increase profits. One can be bourgeois, in the narrow traditional sense, without being a capitalist, and the converse is also true. A capitalist farmer who manages and even works his holding, although he does not necessarily own it, thus is not strictly speaking a bourgeois. Of course, a bourgeois can be a capitalist farmer, but he is not bourgeois from the traditional standpoint by virtue of that activity. There is no reason, however, why the broad, more recent connotation of bourgeois cannot be applied to the capitalist farmer, as E. P. Thompson has occasionally done in writing of the eighteenth-century English agrarian "bourgeoisie."[12] Nor should we hesitate in this broad sense to refer to Locke's bourgeois mentality. Nevertheless, if we combine elements of the traditional and modern meanings, as we are often prone to do, by associating the bourgeoisie with mercantile and manufacturing capitalism in an urban setting, then it seems advisable in the case of Locke and seventeenth-century England generally to refrain from using the term. For the sake of clarity, it may be preferable simply to employ *capitalist* and *capitalism*, specifying, of course, the kind we have in mind.

Locke's life indicates more intimate experience with agriculture than with mercantile and manufacturing activity. He counted important merchants among his friends and associates, invested in various mercantile ventures, dealt with trade in his economic writings, and helped to formulate state policy on commercial matters. His theoretical and practical concern with commerce, however, always forced him to perceive that agriculture was the foundation of English society and should be given the highest priority in all economic considerations and political deliberations. Furthermore, he never vented his wrath on farmers as he did on merchants and monied men. Indeed, on the sole basis of our knowledge of his life and intellectual interests it would probably be more difficult to draft a brief for his being an ideologist of mercantile and manufacturing capitalism than to argue that he was a theorist of early agrarian capitalism. Yet strangely, the role of agriculture in his life and thought has never been emphasized or adequately assessed.

From birth Locke was exposed to farming, and he was always interested in and informed about the subject. The son of a country lawyer, a small gentlemanly landowner and clerk to the Justices of the Peace in Somerset, Locke spent his childhood in a Tudor farmhouse at Pensford, "commanding a magnificent view across the Mendip Hills towards Farmborough and Camerton and Midsomer Norton."[13] This part of Somerset was one of the richer "farming countries" of England, known as the "Western Waterlands," highly reputed among agriculturists. Much of it consisted of drained marsh land, devoted to grass, hay, and grazing and famous for red "Gloucester" cattle, butter, and cheese.[14] Friends and relatives of Locke were landowners in this area of capital farms with convertible husbandry and floating water meadows. After serving in the parliamentary forces, Locke's father returned to be briefly county clerk for sewers,[15] which must have been a position of some responsibility in the marshy farm land of Somerset, for as Kerridge remarks: "Under commissioners of sewers, banks, sluices, sewers, main drains, and other works were both made and maintained."[16] On the death of his father in 1661, Locke inherited the modest landed estate, thus becoming an absentee landlord for the remainder of his life. By Cranston's estimate, Locke in 1669 had been receiving about £240 per year from these properties.[17] This annual income alone was sufficient to maintain a comfortable life for a bachelor gentleman of Locke's modest tastes. Little in the correspondence with his various managers is of moment except to reveal that he was an exacting and impatient proprietor, perpetually exercised by the laxity of his tenants in paying their rents when due.[18]

In 1667 Locke joined the household of Lord Ashley (1621–83), the future first earl of Shaftesbury and lord chancellor. Although better known for his political and mercantile interests, the founder of the Whigs was devoted to husbandry and estate management and was a member of the "Georgical" or agricultural committee of the Royal Society.[19] He owned vast tracts in Hampshire, Dorset, Wiltshire, and Somerset. As one biographer has commented, he possessed not acres but miles of pasture land.[20] His farms were located in the heartland of capitalist agriculture, downlands given to corn and livestock. Joan Thirsk has written of this area: "As early as Henry VIII's reign . . . the downland farmers were engaged in large-scale capitalist farming, which can only have been undertaken with large numbers of wage labourers."[21] Of the Wiltshire chalk country in particular, Kerridge maintains that "by the early sixteenth century, most of the land was in the hands of capitalist farmers, and by the middle of the seventeenth century capital farms occupied most of the farmland."[22] The town of Shaftesbury in Dorset was of more than local standing, with a name in the West for its thriving wool market, grain and cattle trade, and leather fair.[23] Not far away was Lord Ashley's seat of Wimborne St. Giles, fourteen miles southwest of Salisbury, where he planted fruit trees and laid out gardens, developed new strains of apples and plums, and engaged in stock breeding and agricultural experimentation.[24] Locke assisted in these activities, buying trees for his patron and sending him seeds and vines.[25] While residing in France in 1675–79, Locke compiled a little technical work, *Observations upon the Growth and Culture of Vines and Olives: The Production of Silk: The Preservation of Fruits*, which he dedicated to Shaftesbury and presented to him at the beginning of 1680.[26] According to John Hoskins, probably Shaftesbury's solicitor, writing to Locke: "My Lord received it with great joy; and bid me give you a thousand thanks, he perused it greedily, and I see him at it very intent last night again."[27] Shaftesbury's keen interest in farming extended to the New World. One of the Lords Proprietors of the Carolinas, and the moving spirit behind the enterprise, he energetically promoted agricultural innovation in the colony.[28] Again Locke was involved in the scheme as secretary of the Lords Proprietors in 1668–75, and he later performed the same function for the Council for Trade and Plantations under Shaftesbury's presidency. Most important, from 1696 to 1700 Locke was a commissioner of the Board of Trade, an advisory and policy-making body that became the architect of England's mercantile imperialism. In all these positions he participated in the framing of domestic as well as colonial agrarian policy.

In serving Shaftesbury Locke may also have learned much about both domestic and colonial agriculture from two of his benefactor's proteges: Benjamin Worsley and Henry Slingsby.[29] Worsley (d. 1677), a confirmed Baconian publicist on agricultural and colonial problems and years before a friend of Samuel Hartlib and a close scientific associate of Robert Boyle, preceded Locke as secretary of the Council for Trade and Plantations.[30] In Worsley's opinion the size of the population was more important than the extent of territory

for the wealth of the kingdom.[31] He called for enclosure and agricultural reform, and he insisted on the economic benefits of religious
toleration. These were all ideas that became important articles of
faith for Locke. Slingsby (c. 1621–88/90), about whom much less is
known, was the Master of the Mint and a Fellow of the Royal
Society. Secretary of the Council for Plantations, during its brief
existence from 1670 to 1672, he was the patron of John Collins, one
of the originators of "political arithmetic."[32]

Locke's time with Shaftesbury also gave him the opportunity of
putting pen to paper. Some of his efforts touched on agriculture. In
1668 he drafted, at his patron's request, a memorandum entitled
*Some of the Consequences That Are Like to Follow upon Lessening of
Interest to 4 Percent*. The work, which will be examined shortly,
demonstrated his preoccupation with agricultural economics. He also
started in 1669 in collaboration with Thomas Sydenham, the famous
founder of modern clinical medicine, the introduction to a projected
book, *De arte medica*, never to be written.[33] Clearly of Baconian
inspiration, the uncompleted introduction maintains that practical
people like ploughmen and practical inventions are the foundation of
civilized life. Human happiness and well-being owe far more to the
experience and labors of the "dull ploughman" and "unread
gardener" than to all the learned scholars. Our "fair gardens" and
"fruitful fields" are due to these humble workers.

From the time he was an undergraduate at Oxford Locke most
probably came under the influence of an important intellectual tradition that took agriculture very seriously, namely, the ideas of the
Baconian-inspired Puritan reformers of the English Revolution.[34]
Agriculture was, according to Charles Webster, "one of their major
pre-occupations and their extensive writings came to dominate the
literature of this subject."[35] Bacon, of course, had called for the
application of science to agriculture and the writing of natural histories of husbandry as well as of trade. A good proportion of the text of
his *Sylva sylvarum* (1627), published the year after his death, is
devoted to plants, horticulture, sylviculture, agriculture, and agron-
omy.[36] Largely of a derivative nature, these particular sections are
based primarily on Porta's *Natural Magic* and Pliny's *Natural History*. The work as a whole is conceived of as a natural history, a
compendium of facts and observations gleaned from a number of
popular writers. E. J. Russell, at least, having in mind the discussion

of the different agents in the germination and growth of wheat, and the fertility of soil, claims that Bacon had actually conducted experiments and collected some of his data at his country estate.[37]

During the Commonwealth these improvers carried on and advanced the work of the agricultural writers begun in the sixteenth century. Their efforts "contributed towards the acceleration of the pace of agricultural change which was such a conspicuous feature of the second half of the seventeenth century."[38] Among them were Ralph Austen, John Beale, Robert Child, Walter Blith, Cressy Dymock, Gabriel Plattes, Sir Richard Weston, and Benjamin Worsley.[39] The leading and most influential of the agricultural reformers was the remarkable Pole and dedicated Baconian, Samuel Hartlib (d. 1670?). The nucleus of a network of correspondents in the fifties, he concentrated his energies on collecting and publishing data about husbandry, urging government support of agrarian reform, calling for better agricultural education; and with the others he was a prominent spokesman for enclosure. Hartlib was not actually the author of the works on agriculture under his name, to which he only contributed introductions. He was rather the energetic organizer, promoter, and disseminator of agricultural information, who edited and arranged the publication of numerous volumes.

These reformers, who combined a belief in Adam, the tenant farmer cultivating a plenteous Garden of Eden, with the Baconian credo of man's domination of nature, were convinced that agricultural innovation and improvement were fundamental to the creation of a New Jerusalem. They wrote many technical agricultural works and paid much attention to horticulture. Numerous translations of French treatises on horticulture appeared at a time when market gardening was turning into a lucrative enterprise in response to the growing demand for fruit and vegetables by an ever expanding London. Enclosure and improvement of waste and forest lands received emphasis as a means of increasing the food supply and solving the unemployment problem.

One of Hartlib's correspondents observed "that the Genius of this Age is very much bent to advance Husbandry."[40] The truth of the comment is borne out by the fact that the founders of the Royal Society in 1662—luminaries of the stature of Boyle, Robert Hooke, Henry Oldenburg, Petty, John Wilkins, and Wren—shared in this pronounced Baconian concern with husbandry and gardening. The name of Robert Boyle (1627–91) is of particular relevance, for he became the mentor and friend of Locke, who was to be one of his literary executors. In 1646–47 Boyle and Worsley had been the leading lights of the utopian and utilitarian group the "Invisible College," one of whose cardinal aims was the scientific investigation of husbandry, metallurgy, and pharmacology.[41] Indeed, during that brief time, Boyle confessed, his "grand employment" was "to catechise my gardener and our ploughmen concerning the fundamentals of their profession."[42] Writing to his old tutor in Geneva, Boyle advised him to "take the pains to inquire a little more thoroughly into the ways of husbandry, etc., practiced in your parts, and when you intend for England to bring along with you what good receipts of choice books of any of these subjects you can procure, which will make you extremely welcome to our Invisible College."[43] Hartlib knew Boyle and corresponded with him, and he included in his *Chymical, Medicinal and Chyrurgical Addresses* (1655) the virtuoso's first published writing.[44] The initial part of Boyle's important work, *Some Considerations Touching the Usefulnesse of Experimental Naturall Philosophy* (1663), probably written in 1650, reflects the ideals of the Hartlib circle.[45] Boyle, who had made some interesting soil experiments, urged agriculturalists to do likewise on their own lands: "Chymical experiments . . . may probably afford useful directions to the Husbandman towards the meliorations of his Land, both for Corn, Trees, Grass and consequently Cattel."[46]

Locke also knew another important figure among the virtuosi, John Wilkins (1614–72), the future bishop of Chester, whose enthusiasm for agriculture is even less recognized than Boyle's. Not a scientist himself, Wilkins nevertheless was a devoted Baconian with a genius for organizing scientists and promoting scientific causes. He is generally credited with being the guiding light in the founding of the Royal Society, and he became the first co-secretary with Henry Oldenburg. As Warden of Wadham College Wilkins collected a galaxy of scientific greats in the Oxford Experimental Philosophy Club from 1649, at one time or another including Ralph Bathurst, Boyle, Hooke, Oldenburg, Petty, John Wallis, Seth Ward, Thomas Willis, and Wren. Locke and his friend Richard Lower, a prize student of Willis and among the first to perform a blood transfusion, were apparently junior members of this group sometime before 1658.[47] Both Wilkins and the Club gave considerable attention to agricultural matters. Wilkins experimented with wheat in the College Gardens, espoused the cultivation of potatoes as a means of preventing famine, and designed a new plough.[48] One of the major interests of the society seems to have been the culture of fruit trees, an interest that may have been responsible for Ralph Austen's important works on the subject and for Locke's persisting passion for it.

Given Wilkins's fondness for husbandry, it is not surprising that he was a member of the Royal Society's "Georgical" or agricultural committee, instituted in 1664 so that "the best endeavours should be used, to compose as perfect a History of Agriculture and Gardening, as might be."[49] Other fellows associated with the work of the committee included John Evelyn, Dr. Christopher Merrett, Dr. William Croune, Shaftesbury, Boyle, and his friend John Beale, the noted agricultural writer. One of the first efforts of the committee was to gather as much information as possible on differing agricultural practices in the various areas of the country. To this end a detailed questionnaire was drafted, probably the work of Robert Boyle, to be sent to experienced farmers throughout England, Scotland, and Ireland. While generally unsuccessful in obtaining replies, the venture was perhaps the first example of the use of a systematic questionnaire for eliciting data of a technical nature.

Hence Locke, a countryman by birth and upbringing, a Baconian and Fellow of the Royal Society, an associate of Shaftesbury, Worsley, Boyle, and Wilkins, could hardly have failed to be interested in agriculture, a judgment confirmed by his library holdings.[50] As one might expect from Locke's scientific inclinations, his library contained some of the pioneer works of the period on agricultural chemistry. He owned a first edition of Bacon's *Sylva sylvarum* and two later ones. He indexed his copy of the eighth edition of 1664, which he rarely did except in the case of especially valued works. In addition to possessing a copy of J. B. van Helmont's *Ortus medicinae* (1654), of some relevance to agricultural science, Locke had a full collection of Boyle's prolific writings and books by Nehemiah Grew, John Mayow, and John Woodward.[51] Locke also subscribed to the *Philosophical Transactions* of the Royal Society, which contained papers of agricultural import. His interest in husbandry, however, was far from being solely represented by such specialized scientific tomes.

His library comprised a broad range of selections, including the agricultural writers of classical antiquity, farming handbooks, the literature of the improvers, and works on horticulture and botany. Among the ancients were Hesiod, Xenophon, Cato Major, Varro, Virgil, Pliny, Palladius, and the *Geoponika*. He also possessed the 1594 edition of *Rei rusticae libri IV* by the humanist Conrad Heresbach, originally published in Cologne in 1570 and translated by Barnaby Googe in 1577 under the title *Foure Bookes of Husbandrie*. The book introduced the more advanced farming techniques of the Lowlands to England, and it is memorable for its description of a reaping machine and recommendation for the growing of turnips, to become an important innovation in English agriculture. Besides two volumes, *Country Contentments* (1615) and *A Discourse of Hormanship [sic]* (1593), by Gervase Markham, a popular writer of agricultural handbooks, Locke acquired an old standby, Charles Estienne's *Agriculture* (1666), originally published in 1554, translated in 1600 by Richard Surfleet as *Maison Rustique; or, The Countrie Farme* and reissued in 1616 by Markham. Another respected sixteenth-century treatise was a later edition of Leonard Mascall's *The Country-Mans New Art of Planting and Graffing* (1651), largely a translation from French authorities with additional descriptions of Dutch methods.

Of greater significance is Locke's ownership of books either by or containing the treatises of three important agricultural writers of the period: Ralph Austen, Cressy Dymock, and Sir Richard Weston. Austen (d. 1676) was registrar to the Visitors of Oxford, a member of the Oxford Philosophical Club, and a Baconian who compiled an anthology of the lord chancellor's remarks on horticulture. He was represented in Locke's library by *A Treatise of Fruit-Trees* (1657) and by a volume generally attributed to him, although edited by Samuel Hartlib: *A Designe for Plenty by an Universal Planting of Fruit Trees* (1652). Another work issued by Hartlib in Locke's library, *A Discours of Husbandry* (1650), called by Webster "one of the most important agricultural writings of the century,"[52] was a printing of Sir Richard Weston's influential *A Discours of Husbandrie Used in Brabant and Flaunders, Shewing Wonderful Improvement of Land There*, whose authorship was unknown to Hartlib at the time.[53] Weston (1591–1652), a Catholic and royalist Surrey landowner, was a promoter of canal schemes as well as being a noted agriculturist. He was perhaps educated in Flanders, or he at least spent much of his early life there. A version of his classic was also reprinted by Gabriel Reeve in another book owned by Locke: *Directions Left by a Gentleman to His Sonnes for the Improvement of Barren and Heathy Land* (1670). Dymock's proposals for the rational layout of farm land were in still another of Hartlib's compilations: *A Discoverie for Division or Setting out of Land, as to the Best Form* (1653).[54] A Nottinghamshire farmer, Dymock was an inventor, publicist, and proposer of an advanced agricultural college to be established under the Commonwealth. Locke also had a miscellany of writings by various authors published by Hartlib under the title *Of Silkworms in Virginia* (1655). In addition to these, Locke bought many works on economics containing numerous references to agriculture; standard surveys of the countryside by William Camden and Edward Chamberlayne; several books on livestock, among them Sir Roger L'Estrange's *A Treatise of Wool and Cattell* (1677); and over two dozen volumes on horticulture, including William Hughes's *The Compleat Vineyard* (1665) and Francis Drope's *A Short and Sure Guid in the Practise of Raiseing and Ordering Fruit-Trees* (1672). As a physician Locke was attracted to the study of herbs and botany, acquiring more than a dozen books on the subjects, such as the principal works of the pioneer Cambridge natural historian John Ray; the nursery gardener John Rea's *Flora Ceres and Pomona* (1665); two treatises by the apothecary John Parkinson; and the famous catalogue of the Oxford Botanical Gardens by the German gardener Jacob Bobart. Between 1661–65 Locke collected and pressed nearly a thousand specimens from these gardens.[55]

Locke's interest in agriculture is also attested to by the journal he kept of his activities in the years 1675–79, when his close relationship with Shaftesbury was interrupted by a lengthy sojourn in France, ostensibly for reasons of health.[56] As one might expect, Locke commented extensively on medical, theological, and philosophical matters, and he recorded many weather observations. In view of the tendency of some scholars to perceive a connection between his thought and early mercantile and manufacturing capitalism, it is worth mentioning that next to nothing is said about merchants, the bourgeoisie, trade, artisans, urban workers, and very little appears on manufacture. Space is given to taxation, but the most numerous observations—other than on those subjects already mentioned—had to do with agriculture. Forestry, livestock, pastures, meadows, ploughing, fruit, wines, and gardens are treated in detail. The editor of a comprehensive selection from the journal reflects:

If his Journal cannot compare, for wealth of technical detail, with Arthur Young's *Travels in France*, his interest in agriculture made him observe with a keen eye the sights which he encountered as he travelled through the countryside. . . . In Languedoc, especially during his stay at Montpellier, he made copious notes on the cultivation of corn, vines and olives, interrogating the peasants he came across in the fields as to the reasons for the different operations which he saw them carrying out. During his later travels he seldom failed to note down in the Journal the character of the country he traversed, its crops and its prosperity or poverty.[57]

Locke had a keen eye for the widespread rural poverty, the miserable conditions of the peasants resulting from their having to carry a disproportionate share of the burden of the land tax or *taille*.[58] Because of the impoverished circumstances of the people and the lack of money in circulation, he stressed, land rents had fallen by over 50 percent.[59]

Locke's correspondence in France and afterward in both England and Holland suggests more than a casual concern with husbandry and gardening. From his friends he obtained news about botanical works and treatises on plants and acquired some of them for his library.[60] He was constantly receiving seeds of all sorts from friends and in turn sending seeds to them,[61] and he frequently exchanged seedlings, cuttings, and grafts of trees as well as information about silviculture.[62] He offered his close friend and fellow Whig, Edward Clarke of Chipley, advice on the planting of trees along the walks of his country house,[63] and he bought sheep for him in Holland, which he shipped from Rotterdam.[64] At the Masham estate of Oates, where he spent much of his last years, he seems to have taken an active and enthusiastic part in the gardening,[65] priding himself on his apple trees.[66] One of Locke's favorite persons was John Barber, Clarke's gardener at Chipley.[67] Barber's name is often mentioned in the correspondence with Clarke. Locke possessed Barber's paper on yew trees, and he recommended to him a particular method for drying plants. No wonder that in his letters to Clarke, which were to be the core of *Some Thoughts Concerning Education*, Locke recommended for scientific reading to those with a practical rather than a speculative bent the works of Robert Boyle and of "others that have writ of husbandry planting and gardening and the like."[68] At the beginning of 1688 he proposed gardening and grafting as an appropriate recreation for Clarke's heir, if he were to remain at Chipley, for in so doing "he will be able to govern or teach his gardener."[69] While in Holland a letter of November 1686 from Clarke about the removal of

Locke's possessions refers to his "minutes of œconomy and husbandry" and "minutes of Œconomy Husbandry."[70] Although these "minutes" have not so far been identified, they might possibly have included notes on agriculture taken by Locke during the two previous decades that could have been used in the preparation of the memorandum of 1668 and chapter 5 of the *Second Treatise*.

Locke's concern for agriculture and related subjects, of course, should not be exaggerated. Agriculture was never accorded the high place in his life and works given to philosophy, theology, politics, medicine, natural science, and economics. He never wrote a treatise on husbandry, nor did he ever pretend to be a skilled practitioner like Edward Clarke. Nevertheless, there can be little doubt, on the basis of the evidence so far presented, about the vital importance of agriculture in Locke's scheme of things. The fact that his interest in husbandry has been neglected by commentators leads one to assume that they may also have overlooked salient features of his writings. In terms of the evidence, it appears simply inconceivable that a thinker of Locke's vast practical knowledge, penetrating intellect, and acute powers of observation would have been completely oblivious to the significant changes occurring in the agrarian sector, or that he would have failed to respond to them in his social and economic writings. With this problem in mind, our task will be to subject a selection of those writings to close scrutiny.

CHAPTER THREE

The Context of
Economic Ideas: 1668–92

Locke's interest in agriculture is further manifested in the economic writings that are at the core of his social and political theory. His basic economic ideas were first expounded in the memorandum of 1668, and they remained unchanged in their extended form published a quarter of a century later.[1] In the preface to the 1692 volume he unequivocally stated that his early ideas had not altered: "I find not my thoughts now to differ from those I had near twenty years since: they have to me still the appearance of truth."[2] This point is eminently worth remembering because anything written by Locke between 1668 and 1692 on the nature of society, the economy, and agriculture must be read, interpreted, and evaluated—if our understanding of his thought is not to be distorted—within the overarching context of those economic ideas. Oddly, this particular realm of discourse, as well as that of the Baconian agricultural reformers, has been neglected by historians of political thought in examining the *Second Treatise*, especially chapter 5, "Of Property." If the meaning of the *Second Treatise* is to be grasped as fully as possible, therefore, it must be read within these contexts of ideas, in addition to other contexts such as those of the natural law discourse of the age,[3] and the Exclusion tracts of the Whigs.[4] The economic ideas and the reformers' discourse are also essential connecting links between the doctrine of the *Second Treatise* and structural changes occurring in English agrarian society. A deeper appreciation of those major developments and of their relationship to the *Second Treatise* will perhaps reveal it to be neither solely a part of natural law discourse nor a *pièce de circonstance* but a work of more universal significance, a perceptive social document that will illuminate what was actually happening in England, suggesting for us, with the benefit of hindsight, something of the future. After all, this is one way of defining a masterpiece in the history of political thought.

At the outset, Locke's general framework of economic ideas, within which he made his more specific economic recommendations from 1668 to 1692, must be summarized.[5] In 1667 he had drafted an essay on toleration, the forerunner of the famous *Epistola de Tolerantia* (1689), evidently also under Shaftesbury's liberating influence. In the manuscript Locke refers to the "welfare of the kingdom, which consists in riches and power, to this most immediately conduces the number and industry of your subjects," and again at the end he mentions "the number and industry of your people, on which depends the power and riches of the kingdom."[6] These assumptions are not repeated, although they seem to be taken for granted, in the 1668 memorandum. There, however, Locke, who was concentrating on technical matters, voiced other basic economic beliefs. Money in circulation drives the "several wheels of trade"[7]; idle money proportionately lessens trade. The value of exports should exceed imports in order to increase the money supply. The productive sectors of agriculture and manufacturing should be encouraged, and a general level of "frugality and industry" would prevent an influx of cheap foreign commodities.[8] Later, in the *Journal* for 1674 he commented:

> The chief end of trade is riches and power, which beget each other. Riches consists in plenty of moveables, that will yield a price to foreigners, and are not likely to be consumed at home, but especially in plenty of gold and silver. Power consists in numbers of men, and ability to maintain them. Trade conduces to both these by increasing your stock and your people, and they each other.[9]

Subsequently, in the *Second Treatise* and in the *Letter on Toleration*, Locke, from his fundamental economic perspective, saw the protection of citizens and their possessions to be inseparable from the problem of security against hostile nations.[10] After all, the international arena is a state of nature—with all its "inconveniencies"—that at any moment might, in part at least, degenerate into a state of war. The single answer to the related concerns of internal and external security is in the power of the state, which, in addition to military strength and skill, entails a prosperous economy with a favorable balance of trade drawing in the gold and silver of the world. Or as he had put it in 1692:

> Riches do not consist in having more gold and silver, but in having more in proportion than the rest of the world, or than our neighbours, whereby we are enabled to procure to ourselves a greater plenty of the conveniencies of life, than comes within the reach of neighbouring kingdoms and states, who, sharing the gold and silver of the world in a less proportion, want the means of plenty and power, and so are poorer.[11]

Power depends ultimately on riches, and for England wealth means a favorable balance of trade. An English economy necessary for a comfortable survival in a world of competing sovereign nations requires a thriving agricultural infrastructure, a growing manufacturing sector, a large and vigorous labor force in both, and propertied classes of energy, initiative, and thrift, able to accumulate and invest their capital safely and prudently in productive enterprise.

The role given to government in this outlook was to guarantee an environment of peace, toleration, and security at home favorable to the accumulation of capital and business transactions.[12] Regulation of property might be necessary for the public good and is justifiable, providing it is done in accord with the principle of consent, the rule of law, and the law of nature. The state should uphold the value of money, carefully regulate the coinage, never resort to a policy of debasement, allow interest rates to seek their natural level, and keep careful watch over the balance of exports and imports. Through taxation and control of imports productivity might be properly encouraged. A rational colonial policy with regulative acts such as the navigation laws would guarantee sources of raw materials, stimulate home shipping and ancillary industries, and prevent competition with home markets. Finally, a disciplined, industrious, and skilled work force could be developed through an adequate poor law and the provision of institutions for training the unemployed.

The 1668 memorandum was probably written at the request of Shaftesbury, then chancellor of the Exchequer and president of the Board of Trade.[13] Locke's effort was aimed against a project then being widely discussed in governmental circles, which was professed most convincingly by Josiah Child in *Brief Observations* (1668): that the interest rate should be lowered to 4 percent. The position chosen by Locke to defend was that the interest rate should not be set by law and that the value of money should depend on the market. Any other policy, he thought, would adversely affect English trade. Our purpose in looking at the work will not be to recapitulate and analyze Locke's argument or to judge its merits against Child's stand, matters that have already been well discussed by economic experts. Instead, we will stress some commonly neglected features of the essay, and we will search for evidence entitling Locke to be called a theorist of early agrarian capitalism, delineating the main differences between the tracts of 1668 and 1692 from this point of view, with the object of elucidating chapter 5 of the *Second Treatise* as a text within this specific context of economic ideas.

The question of the intellectual origins of the ideas of the memorandum of 1668 (and of the 1692 treatise) still remains to be seriously examined by scholars, a project that cannot be attempted here. Locke may very well have acquired some of his most important economic ideas from William Petty, whose 1667 imprint of *A Treatise of Taxes and Contributions* he owned.[14] Such conjecture, however, cannot ignore Schumpeter's comment: "The superior quality of his [Petty's] mind shows in all his comments and suggestions, but there is nothing very striking or very original or very distinctive about them: they represented the views that were then current, or rapidly becoming current, among the best English economists."[15] At any rate, Petty's opinions would have provided authoritative support for what Locke may have gleaned from the economic discourse of the period.

The two works of Petty and Locke are examples of Baconian natural history, a connection that is not as bizarre as it may seem. In his later writings Bacon maintained that the foundation of true natural philosophy should be natural history, consisting of the systematic and detailed collection of data derived from observation and experiment.[16] Specific attention is to be given to the natural processes of generation, development, and change over time. The procedure was taken up enthusiastically by Bacon's followers in the study of animals, plants, minerals, astronomical bodies, geographical features and regions, diseases, and anatomy; and its promotion became the official policy of the Royal Society. But Bacon did not restrict natural history to such phenomena alone. He was also deeply interested in the compilation of histories of the mechanical arts, and he wished to see the method applied to politics as well as to a wide range of psychological experience. During the Commonwealth period the associates and friends of Samuel Hartlib devoted much of their efforts to gathering information on trades and husbandry. Out of this prodigious industry came the many writings of the agricultural improvers. That the method of Baconian natural history might be used to analyze the constituents of the state was one of Hartlib's germinal suggestions.[17] One of his early collaborators, Petty laid the foundation of the science of political economy with the publication of his *Treatise* of 1662. Petty's Baconian interest in the natural history of society and state, based on the analogy between the *"Body Natural"* and the *"Body Politick,"* culminated in *Political Arithmetick*, possibly written about 1672 but not published until 1690.[18] Baconian natural history as it evolved in the second half of the seventeenth century, therefore, came to include the examination of society as well as nature, thus transforming the sciences.

Methodologically, Locke's memorandum and Petty's *Treatise* are cast in the same Baconian mold, but neither is an ordinary Baconian natural history. Locke's paper, it can be argued, is no less an early example of "political arithmetic" than the book of Petty, who was later to coin the term, if not to invent the idea.[19] Locke, indeed, might appropriately be included with Petty, John Collins, John Graunt, William Potter, and Robert Wood as one of the pioneers of political arithmetic. Their books were in Locke's library. By 1668 several editions of Graunt's *Natural and Political Observations upon the Bills of Mortality* (1662) had appeared, and Potter's books had been published in the fifties, as had Collins's *An Introduction to Merchants' Accounts* (1652).[20] Wood's views on decimal currency and monetary theory were probably familiar.[21] Locke "certainly knew Petty," according to Laslett,[22] was evidently acquainted with Wood,[23] and could possibly have met Collins through Henry Slingsby.[24]

The 1668 memorandum, broadly speaking, shares in the method of the political arithmeticians. Emphasis is given to the empirical examination of social relationships. Numerical observation in terms of the well-known canon of *"Number, Weight, or Measure"* is central.[25] Statistical data were virtually nonexistent at the time, but the quantitative could be estimated and presented as a basic presupposition in the form of an intelligent guess or a calculation from which inferences might be made, what Charles Davenant was to call "reasoning by figures."[26] This procedure typified Petty's works, for, in the absence of precise numerical economic and demographic data, he was never at a loss to make commonsensical estimates, which sometimes proved to be erroneous. Graunt, of course, had the advantage of being able to use parish records in his examination of the City of London mortality rates, but Petty and Locke, given their economic interests, were not in such a fortunate position. Locke's memorandum abounds with such speculative calculations, which serve as points of departure for chains of numerical deductions. A sample of such initial presuppositions is the following: "For supposing two millions of money will drive the trade of England"; "For suppose £10,000 were sufficient to manage the trade of Bermudas"; "For supposing I let a farm at £52 per annum"; "For supposing [that in the year] I Henry VII, N. let 100 acres of land to A. for 6d. per annum per acre rack rent."[27]

Both Locke's memorandum and Petty's *Treatise* were based on shrewd practical observation, eschewing scholastic argumentation and reference to venerable authority. Both were characterized by a probing, analytic approach that attempted to weigh the debits and credits of various economic policies in the manner of double-entry bookkeeping, then concluding with a set of prescriptions in a manner similar to the computation of a final balance. Petty's later description of his essentially Baconian approach in *Political Arithmetick* could easily have described the procedures of his *Treatise* and Locke's memorandum:

> The Method I take to do this, is not yet very usual; for instead of using only comparative and superlative Words, and intellectual Arguments, I have taken the course (as a Specimen of the Political Arithmetick I have long aimed at) to express my self in Terms of *Number, Weight*, or *Measure*; to use only Arguments of Sense, and to consider only such Causes, as have visible Foundations in Nature; leaving those that depend upon the mutable Minds, Opinions, Appetites, and Passions of particular Men, to the Consideration of others.[28]

No brief statement could better illustrate the two thinkers' opposition to the scholastic use of syllogism and maxim, or their emphasis upon quantity and calculation and their reliance on the testimony of sensory experience. Bacon's doctrine of the idols is even invoked as advice to those of equally rigorous inclination.

How, then, did the political arithmeticians conceive of the purpose of their endeavors? It was to provide an empirical foundation and guide for a rational state policy, which for Graunt would "preserve the Subject in Peace and Plenty."[29] He, along with the others, believed that such exact knowledge was "necessary, in order to good, certain, and easie Government, and even to balance Parties and Factions both in Church and State."[30] Clearly, they thought that civic order could only be firmly established and securely maintained by an enlightened public policy informed by practical observation and a sound grasp of social reality instead of metaphysical speculation. This was precisely the kind of policy Davenant had in mind in his classic definition of political arithmetic, one with which Petty and Locke would no doubt have been in agreement and one that characterized their own efforts:

A great statesman—by consulting all sort of men, and by contemplating the universal posture of the nation, its power, strength, trade, wealth and revenues, in any counsel he is to offer—by summing up the difficulties on either side and computing upon the whole, shall be able to form a sound judgment and to give right advice; and this is what we mean by Political Arithmetic.[31]

Often naive, imprecise, and circumscribed in its formulations by the paucity of quantitative evidence, political arithmetic nevertheless was the origin of eighteenth-century political economy and the beginnings of a science of public policy.

Substantively, a number of striking parallels can be found in Petty's *Treatise* and Locke's memorandum. Petty's definition of the function of money "to drive the Nations Trade,"[32] his stress on labor as the primary source of value,[33] and his sense of the vital role of land and agriculture in the "wealth of this nation"[34] were echoed in Locke's work. Also of importance was Petty's focus on the nature of rents[35] and on agrarian structure in terms of landlord, tenant, and laborer with their respective incomes of profits, rents, and wages[36]—both of which were central to Locke's memorandum. Petty as well as Locke took it for granted that the laborer was a low species of being who would receive only subsistence wages.[37] Locke apparently followed Petty in labeling retail merchants "gamesters"[38] and in using the bushel of wheat as the standard unit of value.[39] Petty's references to the dependence of a nation's wealth on the size of population rather than on the extent of territory[40] and to the desirability of agricultural development,[41] entailing technical innovation and the intensive application of labor, had become part of

Baconian conventional wisdom. Although these notions did not appear in the memorandum, they possibly served to bolster what Locke came to realize and make his own some dozen years later in chapter 5 of the *Second Treatise*.

To the casual reader of Locke's memorandum, one of its most noticeable features is the large proportion of space given to questions about land, the landholder, tenants, and agricultural workers. Locke divided the kingdom among the "landholder," the "labourer" (workers and manufacturers), and the "broker" (merchants and shopkeepers).[42] The landholder's lands "afford the materials," the laborer "works them," and brokers "distribute them." Land is the basis of the system of trade because it "produces naturally something new profitable and of value to mankind."[43] Locke was well aware that English landed estates at home and in the colonies were the primary source of the raw materials necessary for economic activity and the wealth of the nation: not only those necessary for food and drink but also wool, flax, silk, and cotton for cloth; weld, woad, madder, and saffron for dyes; flax, linseed, rape, and coleseed for oil; hides for shoes and leather goods; hemp for rope; wood, peat, and coal for fuel; timber, sand, stone, and clay for buildings, ships, naval stores, furniture, and household wares; and ores for the metal industries.[44] The role of the landholder is absolutely crucial; his "interest is chiefly to be taken care of, it being a settled unmoveable concernment in the common wealth,"[45] a conviction repeated in 1692,[46] where it received even greater emphasis: "The landholder, who is the person, that, bearing the greatest part of the burthens of the kingdom, ought, I think, to have the greatest care taken of him, and enjoy as many privileges, and as much wealth, as the favour of the law can (with regard to the public-weal) confer upon him."[47] When Locke discussed the laborer, he usually had in mind the worker on the land. Locke's agricultural orientation is further confirmed by his acceptance in both works of the bushel of wheat as the basic unit of value, the "standing measure" in England.[48]

If land, the landholder, and the agricultural laborer represented for Locke the *sine qua non* of the English economy, he was highly critical of the unproductive section, which he defined as consisting primarily of the class of brokers. Because they removed money from circulation without producing anything of their own, they threatened the system, or so Locke maintained. Trade, and hence wealth and power, depended on the constant unimpeded circulation of money. The "multiplying of brokers hinders the trade of any country."[49] They "eat up too great a share of the gains of trade," with the dire consequence "of starving the labourer and impoverishing the landholder." Unproductive shopkeepers were little better than "gamesters." On this score, Locke's attitude had not changed in 1692; if anything he had become more perturbed by these subversive drones.[50] The landholder, he then contended, must always bear the ultimate economic burden. By keeping up prices for their own narrow economic advantage, greedy brokers bring suffering to the countryside and its inhabitants: landholders, tenants, and laborers. He saw that the major conflict of interest was between landholders and brokers[51] and that any tax other than on rents would in the long run victimize the landed proprietor, forcing him to lower rents, resulting in a decline in land values.[52] So Locke felt that landholders should directly shoulder the tax burden. In spite of this, they could prosper by displaying industry, initiative, and frugality. Land values would not fall, and the economy as a whole would flourish. While in 1668 and 1692 the unproductive middleman was severely taken to task, every incentive, Locke believed, should be given to artisan and manufacturer, particularly to those who merchandized their own products.[53] He seems to have had in mind not large manufacturers—and at the time there were very few of them in England—but petty producers, small and middling craftsmen-merchants. The artisan withdrew less money from circulation than the trader and merchant because his major cost of production was labor—a view borne out by the actual practice of the day—and because he was creating something of use. Locke's stress on the critical economic function of the landholder and his objections to the unproductive role of the broker would hardly substantiate his being called a spokesman for mercantile capitalism. Nor could Locke easily be connected with the rise of industrial capitalism, given his fondness for the petty craftsman, the producer who sold his own wares.

If Locke cannot properly be termed a theorist of mercantile or industrial capitalism, his economic thought in 1668 and 1692 foreshadowed some of the important elements of the eighteenth-century science of political economy, central to which was the capitalist approach to agriculture. His notion of the interdependence of the system of trade on a nationwide basis was a rudimentary conception of the "economy." The analytic, calculating approach to profit and loss, to land values, rents, and labor costs, weighing all variables in terms of short and long-term advantage and disadvantage, and the premium placed on productivity rather than distribution invoked something of the "spirit of capitalism," as did his insistence that land values depended basically on the tenants' output. Needless to say, neither Locke nor his contemporaries had any very adequate conception of "capital," but they did anticipate the idea by using such terms as "stock" and "fund."[54] So in 1692 he contrasted agrarian England, "whose great fund is land,"[55] with mercantile Holland, "a country, where the land makes a very little part of the stock of the country. Trade is their great fund."[56]

A clearer indication of the capitalist aspects of Locke's economic thought, however, is the expression of basic changes occurring in the social relations of English agricultural production, changes that were essential to agrarian capitalism. The first of these is that of agrarian organization in terms of the triad—so beloved by later political economists—of landholder, tenant, and laborer, each with their incomes in rents, profits, and wages.[57] How Locke related this trinity of landholder, tenant, and laborer to his other triad of landholder, laborer, and broker is by no means clear. From the standpoint of source of income one might assume that he would place the tenant in the category of "broker," which is certainly not the case. Because Locke's "landholder" would seem to have been a proprietor or owner living on rents, the tenant deriving his income from profits does not readily fall under that rubric either. Yet we know (as did Locke) that in practice landlords frequently farmed part of their land and that small tenants often worked their holdings without the help of wage laborers. In the first case the income would have been a mixture of rents and profits, in the second, one of profits and wages (money saved from not employing laborers). Moreover, larger tenants might also have undertenants and consequently would receive rents in addition to profits. Locke in *1692* briefly introduced the notions of "landlord and landholder" (given as an example under *landholder* in the *O.E.D.*), "lord of the fee," "under-tenant," "chief rent."[58] So he seems to have recognized some of the problems, even if he did not clarify them. Adam Smith avoided these difficulties by simply speaking of those who receive rents, profits, and wages as composing the "three great, original and constituent orders of every civilized society," and acknowledged the existence of mixtures. He dispensed

with the ambiguous *landholder* in this connection and employed *landlord*, designating anyone receiving rent from real property. For
Smith, then, the tenant who lived on profits was included in the same
order as merchants and manufacturers.[59]

The other reflection of a basic change in the social relations of
agricultural production, subsumed by the triad of landholder, tenant, and laborer, is the wage relationship, and a conception of labor
as a commodity. In reference to the triad, Locke believed that the
more profitable the tenant's operation, the higher the rents and cor-
respondingly the land values.[60] In other words, to use Marxist terminology, the increase of the landlord's income from rents was proportionate to the surplus value created by the laborer, which in turn
rested on the tenant's efforts to increase productivity and reduce
costs. The tenant's profits depended on two basic factors, according
to Locke, providing his costs remained unchanged. He must produce
more where the demand for the commodity remained the same, or he
must produce the same when the demand increased.[61]

What of the laborer in the triad? Locke used the term *labourer* in
two senses: generically, to include all manual workers; and specifically, to refer to farm laborers.[62] When he wrote explicitly about
"manufacturing" laborers, he used the words *artizans, workmen,
artificers, handicraftsmen*.[63] When he had the farm laborer in mind, he
seemed to be thinking primarily of the "day labourer,"[64] not the
"servant in husbandry." The word *servant* seems to have been employed only twice in the whole corpus of his technical economic
writings, and those two instances were confined to the treatise of
1692.[65] There he spoke of "great mens menial servants," and he then
explained that servants like children depend immediately on the
landholder, whose rents maintain them. From what he said, it appears that these servants were "consumers," relatively few in number, and not producers like farmers, laborers, and artisans.[66]

His use of *labourer* to designate explicitly the agricultural laborer
seems to have conformed to traditional usage. The *laboratores*, the
third of the three medieval estates, in contrast to the other two estates
of *bellatores* and *oratores*, were those who engaged in agricultural
work, and they were customarily identified with the peasantry, although other kinds of workers were not necessarily excluded.[67]
Moreover, one principal meaning of the verb *to labour*, common in
seventeenth-century England but now poetic or archaic, was "to
labor on the soil, to till, or to cultivate."[68] While Sir Thomas Smith

used *labourer* or *servant* generally to designate all manual workers,[69] he at least in one passage seemed to differentiate laborers ("day labourers") as agricultural workers from "artificers" such as "Taylers, Shoomakers, Carpenters, Brickemakers, Bricklayers, Masons &c."[70] As with Locke, Petty conformed to this usage, employing *labourer*, in addition to the broad sense, to refer specifically to the farm worker.[71] He called tin miners "workmen" and manufacturing workers "artizans," and like Locke he never considered servants in husbandry.[72]

When Locke discussed agriculture he specified the "day labourer" who was paid by the tenant for his labor power during a fixed period of time.[73] Such workers, he stated, were commonly paid by the week on Saturday night, perhaps a shilling a day, or a total of six shillings per week. We know that day laborers, the conditions of whose labor were fixed by statute, ordinarily worked a dawn-to-dusk day of twelve hours or more, with extra time for dinner, rest, and in summer for sleep.[74] They were distinguished from the two other types of workers in seventeenth-century English agriculture, "servants in husbandry" and "token workers" or "task workers."[75]

Servants in husbandry were young men and women, between the ages of fifteen and twenty-four, who were serving a kind of agricultural apprenticeship.[76] Sometimes from the better rural families, they contracted on a yearly basis with the master, lived in the household as a part of the family, and in addition to board and room received a small remuneration amounting to several pounds a year, often paid as "wages" at regular intervals, for example quarterly, during their period of service. The women usually worked in the dairy, with cows and with poultry, while the men took care of the larger animals and sheep, ploughed, carted, and harrowed. Task work, often of a skilled nature such as ditching and hedging, involved payment for performing a particular task or service. Nowhere in his two economic treatises does Locke ever refer to the task worker in agriculture. By the nineteenth century both servants in husbandry and task workers were disappearing from the rural scene, being replaced by day laborers. In Locke's time servants in husbandry tended to be the characteristic form of farm labor in the north and west, whereas day laborers were the preferred agrarian workers in the more advanced agricultural regions of the south and east.

Instead of exchanging a commodity or service for a stipulated amount, Locke's day laborer sells his labor power to the employer for a mutually agreed time, and all that is produced during that time is the property of the employer. Each party to the contract becomes the owner of what he receives in the exchange: the laborer, his wages; the employer, the product of the labor power during the allotted time. The laborer seeks to sell his labor power to the highest bidder. So, Locke warned, because of the shortage of day laborers in the countryside at the time he was writing, they could always impose their rate of pay on the tenant farmer.[77] Hence, "they must be humoured, or else they will neither work for you, nor take your commodities for their labour." We are left in no doubt in either the works of 1668 and 1692 or in *Further Considerations Concerning Raising the Value of Money* (1695) that, in dealing with the supply and demand for labor in general, Locke was thinking of fairly mobile workers who, far from being tied down out of sentiment or tradition to a particular locale or estate, would go where they would receive the highest price for their labor power, even abroad if necessary.[78]

Locke took for granted, as did his peers, that day laborers were an inferior species of human being, the lowest on the English social scale. Sir Thomas Smith had written that workers and those without free land "have no voice nor authoritie in our common wealth, and no account is made of them but onelie to be ruled, not to rule other."[79] A century later Edward Chamberlayne called day laborers the lowest member of the body politic.[80] Certainly English workers avoided day laboring for wages like the plague. Servants in husbandry were of higher status, and when their service was completed some became farmers themselves, turning to day labor only as a last resort. Locke accepted the fact, without complaint or criticism, that laborers would earn barely subsistence wages, "living but hand to mouth."[81] Like so many of his more fortunate contemporaries he thought the division of society between rich and poor to be inevitable. He would have agreed with Petty's dictum: "No Man needs to want that will take moderate pains. That some are poorer than others, ever was and ever will be: And that many are naturally querulous and envious, is an Evil as old as the World."[82]

Locke's position is reflected in part by two passages in the 1692 treatise. First, he recognized that the unequal distribution of land meant that some would be able to live on rents and others would not, implying the permanent existence of the landlord-tenant relationship and, by implication, that of tenant and laborer.[83] Second, by way of illustrating the amount necessary for the trade of England, Locke hypothetically allotted one million pounds each to the three major economic groupings: landholders, laborers and artisans, and brokers ("for their care and pains in distributing").[84] The result of this division, if put into actual practice given what we know of the existing social structure, would mean appreciably less than one-third of the population (landholders and brokers) would have twice as much as the remaining two-thirds (laborers and artisans), a clear expression of Locke's stand in respect to the inequalities in English society. He also apparently believed that the great disparity between the incomes of laborers on the one hand and landholders and brokers on the other would be the most conducive to internal peace and stability because in their efforts simply to survive workers would be less likely to foment discord:

For the labourer's share, being seldom more than a bare subsistence, never allows that body of men time or opportunity to raise their thoughts above that, or struggle with the richer for theirs, (as one common interest) unless when some common and great distress, uniting them in one universal ferment, makes them forget respect, and emboldens them to carve to their wants with armed force; and then sometimes they break in upon the rich, and sweep all like a deluge. But this rarely happens but in the male-administration of neglected, or mismanaged government.[85]

Six years later Locke concluded that the best dike for withstanding such a deluge of popular unrest, in addition to sound economic policies, was greater labor discipline by means of a more severe poor law.[86]

Two points must be emphasized about Locke's conception of the triadic structure of the social relations of production in the English countryside. First, in respect to agrarian labor, Locke was clearly articulating a fundamental characteristic of modern capitalism. He assumed the separation of the agricultural laborer from the means of production, that is, from the ownership of land and the control of land use. The worker was the juridically free man who exchanged in the market his labor power at the highest available price on a short term basis for wages paid by the capitalist tenant farmer.

Second, Locke, contrary to the evidence of rural England, universalized the triad to include all the countryside. One would mistakenly infer from his account that the triad was the norm. What was the origin of his misconception of agrarian structure? The question is pertinent because the triad typified only capitalist social relations of agricultural production in England, and when Locke was writing agrarian capitalism was still not the rule in the rural sector.[87] Capital farms were becoming increasingly important, but small family farmers, importing grain from other areas and using the customary common pastures, still predominated numerically in the country as a whole, although they were concentrated in the pastoral and forest regions of the north, the moorlands of the southwest, the vales of the West Midlands, and the eastern lowlands. Agrarian capitalism had succeeded in monopolizing the specialized corn growing and the mixed corn and livestock countries: the wolds and downlands, the loams and brecks of East Anglia, and the vales and lowland plains. In these regions there was a marked concentration of landownership at the expense of small holders, and being a large tenant farmer was often more profitable than remaining a landowner. One can only conclude that the major capitalist farming countries like the downlands of Wiltshire, Berkshire, Dorset, and Hampshire, parts of Somerset, and lowland Sussex were the most familiar to Locke, and that he simply generalized their situation. Locke mentioned only two agricultural areas by name, both in the 1692 volume: the Isle of Portland, largely part of the Southdown farming country,[88] and Romney Marsh, well known for its capital grazing operations.[89] Whatever the reasons for Locke's distortion of social reality in this way, the significant point is that by universalizing the triad he apparently conceived of English agriculture primarily as involving capitalist social relations of production. He took the triad for granted, never criticized it, nor did he compare it with other forms of agrarian structure.

Locke published *Some Considerations* at the beginning of 1692 at the request of John Somers, M.P., to whom it was dedicated, and who was to be knighted and to become Lord Keeper of the Seal, leader of the Whigs, and virtual chief minister. The reason Somers, in Locke's words, "put me upon looking out my old papers, concerning the reducing of interest to 4 per cent. which have so long lain by forgotten,"[90] was that London merchants were anxious for cheap money, relying on the argument of Sir Josiah Child. His work of 1668 had been reissued in 1690 under the title *A New Discourse on Trade*, with an addition, *Of Raising Our Coin*. Locke contended that the debasement of the coinage should be resisted by the government. As we have seen, he insisted that his economic views of 1668 were basically those of 1692. The published treatise was no more than an enlargement of the earlier ideas.

But in respect to our special concerns, there is one distinctive difference between the two essays. While in 1668 Locke referred briefly to the importance of "general frugality and industry,"[91] and to the dependence of the landlord's rents on the labor and industry of his tenants,[92] this becomes a constant theme in 1692.[93] "Industry," "frugality," "sobriety," "diligence," "thrift" "good husbandry," "good order," "well-ordered trade" were the terms employed by Locke that summarized his agrarian prescription of 1692, as opposed to "lazy," "idleness," "indigent," "extravagant expenses," "expensive vanity," "debauchery," "ill-husbandry," "ill-management," and "mismanaged trade." Landholders must tighten their belts, live within their means, stop craving expensive imported luxury items, and begin to manage their affairs efficiently for their long-term advantage in the form of increasing rents and profits and the prevention of bankruptcy.

In two passages Locke likened a kingdom to a household, which differs only quantitatively in economic matters. The comparison was to be a marked trait of the new science of political economy. Locke reasoned that a country grows rich or poor just as a farmer does, giving the hypothetical example of a farm that covers the whole of the Isle of Portland.[94] The farmer sells in the local markets of Weymouth and Dorchester the produce of his estate—cattle, corn, butter, cheese, wool or cloth, and lead and tin—worth £1,000 per year, and with it he buys £900 of salt, wine, oil, spice, linen, and silks. Should he do this each year for ten years he will have saved £1,000. By being more prudent, however, he would forego spending his profits on imported luxuries, saving £500 per year instead of £100, thus netting £5,000 rather than £1,000 in ten years. Quite different, however, is the conduct of his spendthrift heir, who lives in debauchery and idleness to the neglect of business, wasting the profits of his inheritance on fashionable and unnecessary luxuries, soon losing the estate and ending in a debtors' prison. Locke concluded:

A farm and a kingdom in this respect differ no more, than as greater or less. We may trade, and be busy, and grow poor by it, unless we regulate our expences; if to this we are idle, negligent, dishonest, malicious, and disturb the sober and industrious in their business, let it be upon what pretence it will, we shall ruin the faster.[95]

In his second use of the analogy, Locke again stressed that a kingdom is like a family and that the value of its commodities must not exceed its expenditures.[96] "Ill-management" and "expensive vanity" would only be catastrophic.

The message could not be clearer. The use of the locale of the Isle of Portland, with cattle and corn leading the list of commodities, intimated that he envisioned a capital farm, common to the South Downlands country. His advice reflected the actual behavior expressed in the two widely known personal farming records and accounts of the century, those of the capitalist farmers Henry Best and Robert Loder.[97] Thrift, industry, and efficient management to minimize losses and maximize profits characterized agrarian capitalism. What Locke failed to tell us was how the expanded profits were to be employed, profits which in the case of the actual practitioners like Best and Loder were used for increasing production by improvements and extending the scope of the enterprise, thus enlarging their incomes.

Locke's reasons for belaboring these points in 1692 are obvious from what he asserted in the text. Throughout he called attention, as he did not in 1668, to the current disastrous economic conditions in the agrarian sector, to the decline of land values, and to the fall in rents.[98] From the standpoint of agriculture it was a buyer's market, spelling disaster for the bastion of the economy, the landholder. We know that in the second half of the century rents and prices began to slump, and that from about 1670 to 1710 rents were around 75 percent of their former level.[99] After a short boom in the second decade of the eighteenth century, depressed land values and rents and low prices of agricultural commodities continued until about 1750, when recovery began. Locke compared his own economically gloomy times to the wealth and prosperity of the reigns of Elizabeth and James I, when land values had been high.[100] The period from 1560 to the second decade of the next century was, in fact, one of rising prices, profits, wages, and rents. Locke's contemporaries like Petty, Aubrey, and Timothy Nourse were aware that they lived in an age of agricultural change, believing that the very success of the improvements accounted for the falling rents.[101] The explanation given by Locke does not necessarily conflict with theirs.[102] He thought the basic cause to be "ill-husbandry" due to "a neglect of government and religion, ill examples, and depraved education." The result had been an increase in "debauchery," and "art, or chance, has made it fashionable for men to live beyond their estates."

It is perhaps not accidental that Locke, after coming to this conclusion, began more frequently to use the term *country gentleman* interchangeably with *landholder*.[103] For although the book is a technical work on interest and money, it is also a plea to the English gentry to arise from their slough of corruption and to mend their ways. Locke was not alone in his condemnation of the laziness and extravagance of the gentry. The problem was deemed to be a serious one by his more enlightened contemporaries, some of whom, at least, thought it might best be solved by suitable governmental measures.[104] Among them was a distinguished physician and botanist, Nehemiah Grew, who on his death in 1712 left in manuscript an economic work called by Michael Hunter "a truly remarkable tract."[105] Gambling should be prohibited, Grew recommended, and hunting should be controlled so as to prevent damage to crops.[106] Rather than wasting their days in idle frivolity, country gentlemen might devote their time to "Improving their Estates and Employing their Heads and Purses in some sort of Good Husbandry, Manufacture, or Merchandize."[107]

With the economic problems always in the background, the corruption of the gentry seems to have been one of Locke's major preoccupations in writing *An Essay Concerning Human Understanding* and *Some Thoughts Concerning Education*.[108] In each case the solution was education, the cultivation of the mind, so that the enlightened individual would approach the problems of ordinary life from a dispassionate, rational, calculating, and self-directed perspective. The energizer of Locke's concern was not so much mercantile or manufacturing developments but the transformation of English agriculture during the previous two centuries and his perception of it. If his economic writings did not offer a mature theory of early agrarian capitalism, at least they represented a significant beginning in their reflection of the vital changes in the social relations of agricultural production so basic to the remaking of the English countryside.

CHAPTER FOUR

"Of Property" Reexamined

The *Second Treatise of Government*, Locke's principal political work, probably written in 1681 and published anonymously in 1690, should be read within this context of economic ideas and the basic social changes that inspired them. This recommendation is in general agreement with two recent scholarly judgments, those of E. J. Hundert, who maintains that to discount Locke's economic thought in interpreting the *Second Treatise* "does violence to his own purposes," and of K. I. Vaughan, who concludes that Locke "in his economic and political writings was presenting a consistent, integrated view of society."[1] Here, however, only the lengthy, pivotal, and much discussed fifth chapter, "Of Property," can be dealt with. Locke, indeed, seems to have considered the central subject of the whole of the *Two Treatises* to be property, for in 1703 he recommended it to his cousin Richard King solely as a political work in which "property I have nowhere found more clearly explained."[2] Coming to chapter 5 as we do directly after an examination of the 1668 memorandum, the most obvious characteristic is not simply property but *landed* property.

Locke concentrated his efforts on the origins of private property in land and the emergence of the distinction between private landed property and common landed property. He also attempted to explain the appearance of differentials in landed holdings. His interest, however, was not only in "history" but also in moral justification. His justificatory discourse, recently illuminated by James Tully,[3] belongs to the tradition of natural law discourse developed by St. Thomas,

Francisco Suarez, Hugo Grotius, and Samuel Pufendorf. Nevertheless, my own approach to chapter 5 will differ markedly from Tully's analysis, since I view the language of natural law primarily as the means adopted by Locke rather than the substance of what he has to say. That substance is in essence the broad economic and social position revealed in the 1668 memorandum. To overlook completely this context in favor of that of natural law discourse may very well hinder our understanding of chapter 5. Moreover, it may prove just as shortsighted to view the natural law context to be more than instrumental as to overlook the even wider context to which the 1668 memorandum was a response: the actual agrarian circumstances of Locke's England and the thoughts of the Baconian improvers about them. This chapter, then, will begin with a very concise summary of Locke's doctrine in chapter 5, which will be seen as basically consistent with the context of economic ideas just assessed. At greater length, some of the major themes of chapter 5 will then be related to the discourse of the improvers. My purpose is to suggest that nothing in chapter 5 invalidates the thesis that Locke was a theorist of early agrarian capitalism and that much of what he does say tends to buttress that thesis.

Before summarizing "Of Property," however, it must be related to another context of ideas. It may seem even more bizarre to term the chapter a Baconian natural history than it did to apply the designation to the memorandum of 1668. Nevertheless, this seems to be precisely what the chapter is from the methodological standpoint, and as we shall see later, it bears substantively the unmistakable imprint of the Baconian agrarian reformers. All commentators have recognized the critical role of the chapter, one of the longest of the *Second Treatise*, because of its account of the state of nature, the labor theory of property, and the natural right of property, but none has perceived its Baconian character.

Locke used the idea of the state of nature in both an ethical and an historical sense, the locus of the one being chapter 3, "Of the State of Nature," and that of the other, chapter 5.[4] The historical state of nature of chapter 5 is characterized by change, process, and development. The pronounced dynamic quality arises not so much because of the treatment of the state of nature per se as because of the focus on property, as the chapter title declares, on the development of the institution of private property, within, of course, the sphere of mankind's prepolitical life. The dynamism of Locke's history is due to his labor theory of property. His view that man's entitlement to property depends on "shaping" the raw stuff of nature with his labor seems basically to account for the protean scene presented to the reader, one of constant flux, energy, industry, and ingenuity. This natural history of property begins, just as does Locke's later natural history of the psyche in *An Essay Concerning Human Understanding*, with a *tabula rasa*, a "white Paper, void of all Characters," no doubt following Bacon's own similar expression: "A fair sheet of paper with no writing on it."[5] In this instance the blank tablet is a vast, unproductive, and scantily populated wilderness like America. As Locke said, "In the beginning all the World was *America*."[6] If the world and its fruits were initially, according to Locke, a divine gift to men in common, he justified its subsequent parcelization and privatization by individual labor. The process of change he unfolded was caused by the creative, fabricating powers of men. Something like the following developmental sequence was given by Locke, although not so clearly specified: small primitive population, movable property, landed property, use production, population increase and concentration, barter and money, property differentials, dependent labor, exchange production, social conflict, and the eventual emergence of the state. A rudimentary four-stage evolutionary sequence can also be extracted without too much difficulty from Locke's natural history of property.[7] The four stages, each entailing a different mode of subsistence, are: food gathering and hunting,[8] pastoral,[9] agriculture,[10] and commerce.[11] This, according to Ronald Meek, is one of the important origins of the more fully developed four-stage theory of Adam Smith and classical political economy.[12]

Locke was not concerned only with the natural history of property and its impact on the whole of human life; like all true Baconians, he had a keen eye for the practical utility of his account. Of the twenty-seven sections of the chapter, twenty-two referred to agricultural property and its problems.[13] In effect he was making policy recommendations as he proceeded, in regard to common land, waste land, enclosure, and agricultural productivity. Some nine of the twenty-seven sections referred to contemporary agricultural questions,[14] and three of these exclusively so.[15] In one section, in which he insisted that labor is basically responsible for the value of things, he offered what amounted to a brief, concise natural history of a loaf of bread within his larger natural history of property: from the different kinds of labor necessary to produce the wheat to those involved in the final baking of the loaf.[16] Or as he summarized it: "'Twould be a strange *Catalogue of things, that Industry provided and made use of, about every Loaf of Bread*, before it came to our use, if we could trace them."

Like other Baconian natural historians, Locke never cited or quoted a wide variety of authoritative texts. He could not, however, base his history on observation or firsthand experience for the obvious reason that he was writing about what we would call "prehistory" at a time when archaeological evidence was unavailable, and about a period in the life of man before the existence of written records. He relied extensively in at least nine sections on the biblical account of early man, which he accepted along with his contemporaries as a perfectly valid historical source.[17] In using the Bible to substantiate his history, he was also obliquely replying to Sir Robert Filmer, against whose patriarchal theories the *Two Treatises* were directed and whose interpretation of the biblical story of prehistorical man and society was so markedly different from his own. Moreover, in attacking Filmer both directly and indirectly in this way in chapter 5, Locke as a Baconian natural historian was also waging war against Aristotle and the schoolmen. For after the Bible, Aristotle, "the grand master of politiques,"[18] was a fundamental authority in the works of Filmer.[19] It is clear, nevertheless, that Locke in chapter 5 was resting his natural history of property on other kinds of uncited evidence, for example: the extensive travel literature and accounts of America that described a condition seemingly analogous with the life of man in its original form and, most important, the enormous output of the Baconian agricultural improvers.

The novel quality of Locke's natural history becomes evident if it is compared to the treatment of the state of nature and property in another uncited source that he apparently read in working out some of his own notions about natural law. This was Samuel Pufendorf's *De jure naturae et gentium libri octo*, published in 1672 and owned by Locke.[20] In contrast to his own dynamic history, Pufendorf's exposition tends to be static, wordy, and legalistic, full of numerous, lengthy quotations from and references to a host of ancient and modern authorities, along with complex disputatious arguments with them. Unlike Locke, Pufendorf held that a pure state of nature was a fiction and that it existed originally in the distant past in impure form, between social groupings, the families of the descendents of Adam and Eve, just as it did at a later date between sovereign states.[21] Labor played little or no part in his explanation of private property, and hence the dynamic trait of Locke's history is notably absent. In the original God-given condition of men, Pufendorf argued, the world and its fruits were neither common nor private.[22] All property, however held, depended on the tacit or express covenants of men. Pufendorf seldom distinguished as clearly as did Locke between movable and landed property, nor did he dwell on the questions of agricultural productivity, waste and common land, and enclosure. Primarily for these reasons his analysis tended to be lifeless, archaic, and antiquarian, singularly devoid of the movement and change so typical of Locke's history.

Locke was the first classic political theorist to place such great emphasis on labor, making it the cornerstone of his edifice of political ideas. Thus his thought must be distinguished from the aristocratic predilections of predecessors like Plato, Xenophon, Aristotle, and Cicero; from the medieval outlook; and from the views of previous early modern thinkers like Machiavelli, Bodin, and Hobbes. The *locus classicus* of Locke's conception of labor and its connection with politics was the *Second Treatise of Government*, in particular chapter 5. Man, according to Locke, was created *homo faber* in the image of God, his maker, *deus faber*.[23] The product of the strenuous labor and "workmanship" of God, each man is God's property. The world and its fruits were originally given by God to men in common to be used for their benefit and well-being. In following God's command to subdue the earth by laboring on it, the individual could appropriate what he needed for his own life and comfort from the common storehouse of nature.[24] Therefore, he could legitimately acquire property in the state of nature by means of the work of his own hands, by mixing his labor with anything in nature. Labor was the origin of and entitlement to private possessions and landed property as distinct from what was common. Man had property in his own person, and since labor was an extension of his person, anything with which he mixed his labor became his property by natural right, property to which no one else was morally entitled.

Since his Christ Church days Locke believed that property was protected by divine and natural law. The second commandment prohibited theft, and, unless God expressly enjoined the contrary, the law of nature prescribed "that every man should be allowed to keep his own property" and "that no one may take away and keep for himself what is another's property."[25] Without the common observance of natural law there could be no security for possessions or for the pursuit of self-interest.[26] One of Locke's dearest beliefs was that without private property injustice could not exist.[27] The infringement of what rightfully belonged to an individual was a threat because the object that was his was an extension of his moral being or person through his labor. An individual's life as an animate being, a moral person characterized by labor, was his own property, held in trust from God, and any attempt to damage or destroy without right what belonged to God would be unjust. Self-preservation, by definition entailing the preservation of one's property as well as one's life, was a fundamental law of nature.[28] Therefore, one had the right to all things, within reason, for the maintenance of himself and his possessions. These were his and his alone by the law of nature.

Locke made two fundamental points about the natural right of property in political society as distinguished from the state of nature. First, private property was defined and regulated by civil law. Man, of course, created political society to secure and protect what was his own by the right of nature. Any violation of his natural right to property contravened the law of nature and was morally illicit. Second, the natural right to property in political society, however, was not an absolute right, for it was subject to the common good, the preservation of society being the first and fundamental law of nature, taking priority over self-preservation.[29] Normally, government should not concern itself or interfere with men's souls and opinions; with their sinning in the sense of being avaricious, uncharitable, or idle; or with their domestic affairs, occupations, estates, and health.[30] Nevertheless, the lives and properties of men in political society were definitely subject to governmental control for the public good, providing certain conditions were met.[31] Government could never legitimately deprive an individual of his property or any part of it—the reference was primarily to taxation—without his consent, which for practical purposes meant the consent of the legislature duly elected by a majority.[32] Any legislative action impinging on man's life, liberty, and property must also be in accord with the rule of law and the law of nature and must be aimed at the "publick good," called by Locke "the Foundation and End of all Laws."[33] Nor could a legitimate legislative regulation of property be designed to impoverish subjects.[34] It must be for the preservation of all, of society as a whole, in accord with the first and fundamental law of nature. In this connection, it should not be forgotten that Locke always upheld the legislative right to regulate for the public good indifferent things in religious matters, as the time, place, and manner of worship, and he steadfastly objected to the toleration of doctrines he deemed incompatible with political society.[35]

In the state of nature, the natural right to property was likewise conditional, at least initially, in that it was subject to the moral limitations of the law of nature on individual appropriation from the common storehouse of nature. The first of these was the "labour limitation," that one was entitled to appropriate only what he could acquire by his labor.[36] Man's life, central to which was his moral being or person, was God's property and could not be voluntarily surrendered or sold, although one could forfeit his freedom, that is, be legitimately enslaved as a result of participation in an unjust war.[37] A man could also indenture himself.[38] If a man's life was not alienable, his labor was. The master-servant relationship was as old as history, existing in the state of nature.[39] By means of a free contract an individual could agree to labor for another in exchange for wages (money, produce, service).[40] Under the terms of such a labor agreement, whatever the servant in the course of his contracted duties acquired through his labor became the property of his master. While Locke originally stated that labor was the foundation of property, such labor need not be one's own. Instead, it could be that of another who was employed for the purpose, thereby overcoming the labor limitation on appropriation. The "sufficiency limitation" meant that in the appropriation of the bounties of nature the individual was morally obligated to leave what was as good as he himself had taken and sufficient for the subsistence of others.[41] This was no real problem in the first stages of the state of nature where only a very small scattered population existed in proportion to the abundance of nature.[42] However, with the growth of population and the concentration of human settlement, the sufficiency limitation could be overcome because labor, industry, and improvement could so increase the productivity of land as to multiply substantially the fruits of the earth, thereby providing a plentiful supply for all. Money, further-more, and the enhanced possibility of wage labor resulting from the introduction of money, which enabled people to live without land, were also of aid in surmounting the sufficiency limitation. Finally, the "spoilage limitation" of the law of nature restricted individual appropriation to what one could use for his own preservation and prohibited the spoilage of any surplus.[43] This limitation was even-tually transcended, first by barter and then by the introduction of the convention of money prior to the creation of political society.[44]

The institution of money in the state of nature (following compacts for barter) and tacit agreement as to its value meant that it was possible for men to enlarge their possessions and establish a natural right to them without violating the spoilage limitation. Once this moral prohibition was legitimately overcome, men could accumulate as much property as they desired, commensurate, of course, with the dictates of reason and the common good, with the consequence of an increase in property differentials. Money greatly accelerated the ten-dency (existing before its introduction) for the industrious to acquire more than the less industrious. For Locke believed that God granted the world to men in common, to "the use of the Industrious and Rational . . . not to the Fancy or Covetousness of the Quarrelsom and Contentious,"[45] and the differences in the size of individual possessions arose because of different degrees of industry.[46] The source of productivity was labor and industry.[47] The value of all commodities depended to the most important extent on the labor and industry they embodied.[48] Much more significant than the extent of territory, however, was the number of productive individuals. The use of money accounted for the increase of people and "stock" in some parts of the world and rendered land—unlike America with its vast empty tracts—scarce and valuable.[49] Money also, or so Locke implied, facilitated the use of the labor of others through the pay-ment of wages. Another result of money was the beginning in the state of nature of a division among mankind between property-owning, economically independent heads of households and those who must exchange their labor for wages in order to survive.[50] All of these tendencies in the state of nature developed hand in hand with the impetus given by money to exchange and trade. In some parts of the world, therefore, use production gradually gave way to production for exchange and profit due to money. Initially the whole world was like America, a world of use production without money and trade.[51] Once money had been instituted in certain regions, Locke suggested, men were able to enlarge their possessions and trade with other regions, thereby hoping to draw in money through establishing a favorable balance of trade. In turn, such commerce stimulated industry and effort, increased productivity, enlarged the possessions of some, and enabled the population and labor force to expand. Because of their tacit agreement setting the value of money, men before the establishment of political society consented to the existence of property differentials.[52] Political society was founded in order to secure and protect these differentials arising in the state of nature because no one could be supposed to enter political society with the intention of worsening his condition.[53]

Those unfamiliar with seventeenth-century English society may not recognize that much of the language of chapter 5 was that of the agricultural improvers. Locke's emphasis was always on increasing the productivity of land by labor and industry. After quoting in the *First Treatise* the command of God, Genesis 1:28, *"Be fruitful, and multiply, and replenish the Earth,"* Locke explained that it included "the improvement too of Arts and Sciences, and the conveniences of Life."[54] In the *Second Treatise* Locke affirmed that God directed man "to subdue the Earth, *i.e.* improve it for the benefit of Life."[55] He who complied with God's wishes "subdued, tilled and sowed" some part of the earth. Furthermore, since "God gave the World to Men in Common . . . for their benefit, and the greatest Conveniencies of Life they were capable to draw from it, it cannot be supposed he meant it should always remain common and uncultivated. He gave it to the use of the Industrious and Rational."[56] Whatever else was entailed by the divine fiat, as interpreted by Locke, it clearly and distinctly required men to enclose and cultivate the earth for their benefit, and those who did so industriously and rationally, it would seem, were especially blessed in God's eyes.

Locke's language is similar to that of the seventeenth-century English agricultural reformers for whom God's injunction in Genesis was a favorite justification in their call for enclosure and utilization of waste land.[57] God was the "Great Husbandman" who had cursed the earth because of Adam's sin and had condemned him and all human kind to lives of ceaseless labor on the barren land.[58] Human redemption, thenceforth, depended on transforming the original waste of the world into fruitful and productive acreage. By art, that is, agricultural labor, man through divine grace was capable of subduing nature and creating a "new world."[59] Such cultivation of the land, John Evelyn stressed, "is indeed of large and profitable extent, though it be but poor and mean in sound, compared to mines of gold and silver, and other rich ores, which likewise are the treasures of the Earth, but less innocent and useful."[60] Robert Boyle has left us with an eloquent eulogy to the usefulness of the earth and its transformation by the art of man:

The Earth produces him an innumerable multitude of Beasts to feed, cloath, and carry him; of Flowers and Jewels to delight and adorn him; of Fruits, to sustain and refresh him; of Stones and Timber, to lodge him; of Simples, to cure him; and in summe, the whole sublunary World is but his Magazine. And it seems the grand business of restlesse Nature so to constitute and mannage his Productions, as to furnish him with Necessaries, Accommodations, and Pleasures.[61]

The word *subdue* of the biblical text for these writers was more or less synonymous with the Baconian notion of the domination of man over nature. The "true Naturalist" in Boyle's view was one who not only understood nature but in addition was able to master her by improving and increasing her products.[62] To Boyle and other Baconians the "Empire of Man" over nature was a kind of moral equivalent of war and conquest, and it was preferable to them because it "is a Power that becomes Man as Man," a creature of reason, knowledge, and dignity.[63] Cultivation of the earth and the multiplication of its fruits, therefore, were thought essential to the divinely ordained universal calling of man.

Although Locke's own view may not have been identical with the Baconian ideal of these reformers, very little of what he said was opposed to it, and his vocabulary was often theirs. He employed *subdue* in connection with agricultural cultivation.[64] More significant is his use of the terms *improve, improver, improvement*, which do not appear in Genesis, for they had special relevance to the reformers and projectors. An *improver*, to quote the *Oxford English Dictionary*, was "One who applies himself to making land more productive or profitable." He was one who introduced or applied the technical agricultural innovations devised since the sixteenth century and who increased productivity by enclosure and cultivation of waste land. So the Warwickshire farmer and Parliamentary soldier Walter Blith, an associate of Samuel Hartlib, published in 1649 *The English Improver, Or a New Survey of Husbandry*. Later editions of the book in 1652 and 1653 were entitled *The English Improver Improved*. Andrew Yarranton published in 1663 *The Improvement Improved, by a Second Edition of the Great Improvement of Lands by Clover*, and in 1670 there appeared *England's Improvement Revived* by Captain John Smith.[65] Books and tracts with similar titles are too numerous for listing. That the words continued to be popular is testified to by the name "Society of Improvers" given to the first British agricultural organization, founded in Edinburgh in 1723. They were certainly favorites of Locke, who used them nearly a dozen times in chapter 5, for instance: "*As much Land* as a Man Tills, Plants, Improves, Cultivates";[66] the "uncultivated wast of America left to Nature, without any improvement, tillage or husbandry";[67] the "improvement of Pasturage, Tillage, or Planting."[68] The ultimate object of improvement and the increase of agricultural productivity was the "benefit of Life," and in the process the value of individual landed holdings were enhanced.[69] Labor, industry, and "Invention and Arts" (scientific husbandry) were the chief means of improvement.[70]

Locke left no doubt about his opposition to idleness and stressed the importance of labor and industry that would yield higher productivity.[71] Petty's dictum had been: "Labour is the Father and active principle of Wealth, as Lands are the Mother."[72] For the reformers idleness and sloth were the chief obstacles to agricultural improvement.[73] "Study Industry," recommended Blith in a passage that may have inspired Petty, for "Improvement is neither Father nor Mother unto Plenty, but I may say it is the Midwife that Facillitates the birth."[74] Evelyn's advice on labor was that "there is nothing excellent which is to be attain'd without it."[75] Sermons and clerical writings of the period, directed to countrymen, for example, those of Nathaniel Newbury and Richard Baxter, condemned idleness, slothfulness, waste, and extravagance, while extolling industry, frugality, and thrift.[76] God, Locke affirmed, gave the world "to the use of the Industrious and Rational, (and *Labour* was to be *his Title* to it;) not to the Fancy or Covetousness of the Quarrelsom and Contentious."[77] Industry, he believed, was largely responsible for the miraculous production of corn on the barren waste lands of Spain.[78]

The only citation in chapter 5 to a specific English farming area is

to Devonshire, extolled by Locke as an example of how industry and
improvement could transform barren land into fertile acreage.[79] Mar-
garet Campbell mentions various improvers who praised the extraor-
dinary industry of the farmers in that county:

> Devonshire was the shire most often referred to as a shining example of the
> way in which a naturally barren county could become one of the most
> productive through care and treatment of its soil. The husbandry
> "innovators" begged less industrious and less wideawake sections to follow
> Devon's example.[80]

She then quotes William Camden's *Britannia* (1610), a book in
Locke's library, which described Devon land as "leane and barren
which notwithstanding yeeldeth fruit to the husbandman plen-
teously, so that he be skilfull in husbandry, and both can take paines,
and be able withal to defray the cost."[81]

Locke believed that the worth of all commodities was due to
industry, for "*labour makes the far greatest part of the value* of things,
we enjoy in this World."[82] For this reason the prince should protect
and encourage "the honest industry of Mankind."[83] Labor and industry were the origins of property,[84] and they accounted for property
differentials;[85] those displaying the most industry and the greatest
effort would acquire more than those deficient in these respects.
Nowhere in the chapter or elsewhere in his writings did Locke object
to wide disparities in wealth or property. Indeed, he would probably
have sided with most of the improvers that the larger the individual
holdings the more efficient their management and the higher their
productivity. A few dissenters such as Sir Thomas Culpeper, junior,
and Carew Reynel in the sixties and seventies were against the trend,
but they were a distinct and uninfluential minority.[86]

Locke never tired of pointing out that from the standpoint of
productivity the number of men counted for far more than the area
of land,[87] a belief he concisely summarized in a line, added perhaps
about 1698: "Numbers of men are to be preferd to largenesse of
dominions."[88] Obviously, he was thinking of the productive potential
of a large disciplined and industrious labor force that could be put to
work improving the land. Once again he echoed the thought of Petty
and the sentiments of the agricultural reformers.[89] People were the
great stock of the kingdom. Material abundance required a vast labor
force. The two were mutually dependent, and because of this England could easily double her population, or if not, according to the

less extreme formulation of Silvanus Taylor, the enclosure of waste lands alone might feed one-fifth more people.[90] Along these lines of speculation, Carew Reynel offered the opinion in 1674: "If we had but a million more of people than now, we should quickly see how trade and the vend of things would alter for the better."[91] John Houghton "modestly" calculated that England could support an extra two million souls by enclosing the waste land.[92] But no one was more optimistic than Nehemiah Grew, who maintained that "a multitude of hands well employed are Fundamental to the Wealth and Strength of any State."[93] His estimate was that if English land were fully utilized, a total population of fifty-five million would be within the realm of possibility.[94]

Locke's closest connection to the improvers' realm of discourse is revealed by his continuous reference to "appropriation," "enclosure," "common land," and "waste land."[95] At first reading of the text it appears that there were three different types of common land: the world at the beginning of time bequeathed by God to men for their use and benefit; the vast unexploited wilderness of America and other comparable regions in Locke's day; and areas jointly owned by "Country" or "parish" and upheld by civil law, the commons in England.[96] The first two kinds were in fact identical because "in the beginning all the world was *America*."[97] Common land in this sense could be rightfully appropriated by labor and enclosed without express consent of the commoners, but such was not true of commons in the third sense. There, any enclosure could only be undertaken with the agreement of all the commoners.[98] However, in each case the commoner could rightfully take things from the land—water, turf, wood, ore—without the express approval of his fellow commoners. John Evelyn, like most of the reformers, was sceptical of this kind of communitarian arrangement. He was particularly incensed by the resulting indiscriminate cutting of timber trees, and for the sake of conservation he recommended some form of enclosure of such unimproved commons, hitherto laws "in favor of *Custom*, and for the satisfying of a few clamorous and rude *Commoners*, being too indulgent."[99]

Locke then turned to the question of landed property, improvement, and enclosure, introducing the conception of "waste land,"[100] eventually defining it as follows: "Land that is left wholly to Nature, that hath no improvement of Pasturage, Tillage, or Planting, is called, as indeed it is, *wast*; and we shall find the benefit of it amount to little more than nothing."[101] This conformed to the common usage of the period. According to the *Oxford English Dictionary* a *waste* is "uninhabited (or sparsely inhabited) and uncultivated country," and *waste land* is "land in its natural, uncultivated state." Locke's definition is given in the *O.E.D.* under the adjective *waste*. Now it would appear that for Locke common land in the first two senses—the world in the beginning and contemporary wildernesses like America—were basically waste lands. One can also infer from what he said that commons in the third sense—those of joint ownership underwritten by the civil law of a specific country—were likewise waste lands, for he pointed out how much more productive one acre of "inclosed and cultivated land" was than one acre "of an equal richnesse, lyeing wast in common."[102] His single description of an English commons,[103] the much discussed "turfs passage," made no reference to common fields, tillage, cultivation, or livestock. It was simply a barren where a horse could graze, turfs were cut, and ore was extracted. The example he gave of the ocean as "that great and still remaining Common of Mankind,"[104] moreover, may be of interest, because his contemporaries sometimes labeled it a "waste."[105]

Locke, therefore, seems to have thought of unimproved commons as waste land. It should be stressed that in his remarks about commons Locke never apparently had in mind the common fields, still so widespread in his England. In contrast, the commons he considered were uncultivated lands, and hence his use of the pejorative *waste* in describing them. A waste in his view was simply any uncultivated land capable of improvement and agricultural productivity. In this he again was conforming to the widely held opinions of the reformers.[106] Blith in 1649 commented on "those great and vast Commons, called Heaths, Forrests, Moores, Marshes, Meades."[107] Robert Child identified "dry *heathy* Commons" as a "Sort of *waste-land*," although he admitted that the poor who depended for a living on these commons might object to their being so designated.[108] "Too much of *England* being left as waste ground in Commons, Mores, Heaths, Fens, Marishes, and the like, which are all Waste Ground," was a major complaint of Cressy Dymock in 1653.[109] John Evelyn advocated the improvement of wastes by tree planting, especially those that would yield timber.[110] While Child was perturbed by the vast unproductive acreage, he was sceptical of the "common saying" that more waste existed in England than in the whole of Europe.[111] Calculations of the proportion of waste land were numerous. Taking John Graunt's statistic of twenty-five million as a minimum and twenty-eight million as a maximum for total land acreage in England and Wales, John Houghton estimated six million acres of waste.[112] Perhaps less exaggerated than Gregory King's figure of one-quarter as waste[113] was Nehemiah Grew's calculation of one-sixth.[114]

But with a large population to feed and clothe and increasing unemployment, the whole question of wastes, regardless of the accuracy of contemporary assessments of their extent, was a critical one. Joan Thirsk tells us that " 'improvement of the wastes and forests' became the slogan of the age" and that the problem was given priority by the improvers, especially during the Interregnum.[115] The basic aim of Sir Richard Weston's pioneer effort at the beginning of the period was to solve the problem of how English waste might be transformed into highly productive agricultural land by following the example of the farmers of Brabant and Flanders, or as Gabriel Reeve put it in the epistle dedicatory to his edition of the book: "The Design of the ensuing Directions is to render the Barren Earth fruitful."[116] The subtitle of Hartlib's *Discoverie* was *For Direction and More Advantage and Profit of the Adventurers and Planters in the Fens and Other Waste and Undisposed Places in England and Ireland.* Not the least of the considerations of the improvers was the enormous profits to be reaped from rendering wastes productive.[117] Biblical authority was even used to justify improvement of wastes, for it was thought by at least one author, following Isaiah 49:19, that then was the time to follow the injunction: "Wast and desolate places shall be inhabited."[118]

Improvement of the wastes meant for the improvers, as it did for Locke, enclosure. In the seventeenth century "enclosure by agreement" was commonplace, much of it of a piecemeal nature, and some entailing few acres, the land appropriated by the commoners often being in proportion to their own holdings.[119] Formal agreements were sometimes unnecessary. Enclosure without consent was customarily tolerated as long as small areas were involved and the direct interests of the commoners were not blatantly violated. Large proprietors ordinarily welcomed enclosure of their forest and marsh lands, because it would provide a new source of rents. Land-hungry and profit-oriented yeomen were prominent enclosers, often found guilty of violating common rights.[120]

Two of the most prominent means of enclosing and improving waste lands had been fen drainage and disafforestation. Prior to the Civil War period more than £400,000, largely Dutch merchant capital, was spent to drain over one-half million acres in Yorkshire, Lincolnshire, and East Anglia.[121] A syndicate formed by the fourth earl of Bedford invested £100,000 in the most ambitious of these fen-draining projects, the 307,000 acres of the Great Level in Cambridgeshire. For his own share of £15,000 the earl received 12,000 acres, which by 1662 accounted for one-third of his gross landed income. A second example is that of the decisions of the Crown from 1626 to disafforestate and enclose the Royal Forests in Western England and in Worcestershire and Leicestershire, a total area of well over 30,000 acres.[122] These forested commons could, it was thought, be sources of lucrative profit to the Crown if they were transformed into leasable farm lands. Scrupulous procedures were followed in each case, beginning with the appointment of an exchequer special commission that would survey the forest in question, acquire the consent of the commoners, and negotiate compensation for the surrender of their common rights in the form of parcels of the enclosed acreage with the balance—a total of three-quarters or more—reverting freehold to the Crown. Although these instances of fen-drainage and disafforestation were enclosures by agreement of the propertied commoners, they disrupted the traditional way of life of the propertyless cottagers, who depended on the wastes for their very survival. As a consequence widespread civil disturbances and sometimes massive riots of the irate and desperate poor—left with little alternative but to become wage laborers—occurred in both fen and forest country, involving destruction of banks and fences and occupation of the allotments.[123]

Just as conscience-stricken writers of Tudor times adamantly opposed enclosure, so most of the seventeenth-century improvers endorsed it.[124] The glowing account of the advantages given by John Houghton is not untypical:

'Tis Inclosure will make *our Yoaks easie, our Burdens light*; 'tis this will improve our Lands and Mines, and bring in the Linnen Manufacture; 'tis this will fill our Cities and Country Towns, and increase and vend our Woollen Products; 'tis this will bring us our Neighbours Arts, and get us abroad a mighty Correspondency; 'tis this will imploy all our Poor, and shift them from their Shelter and Dens of Laziness; 'tis this may find out some new Discoveries, and encrease and encourage our old Plantations; 'tis this will, by reason of more Consumers, encrease our Fishery, and make us want (instead of complain of) many Ships; and 'tis this will strengthen our selves, and frighten or annoy our Enemies; and why an increase of people 20 or 25 *per Cent.* will not encrease His Majesty's Revenue to almost the same proportion, I want another *Oedipus*.[125]

The foremost argument for enclosure, shared and constantly stressed by Locke, was the enormous advance in productivity. Increase in productivity meant burgeoning profits. An appeal to self-interest was usually made, often cloaked in the guise of the common interest. The farmers' profits would benefit the nation, leading to a general prosperity.[126]

Another principal defense of enclosure had to do with the view that common grazing lands and wastes generated unemployment, idleness, and vagabondage. Fear of "masterless men" who roamed the countryside, acknowledging no authority, and who were "insolent" to their social superiors—always a plague to landlord, church, and government—seems to have haunted the propertied classes throughout the ages.[127] Enclosure would provide permanent employment for such people, putting an end to their vagrancy, and it would place them under the watchful eye of landholder and magistrate. In the process, of course, the land would become more fruitful. Some of the reformers were particularly insistent that poor commoners should not be disadvantaged by enclosure and that in order to prevent this an equitable division of the lands should be ensured.[128] Their objective seems to have been, in the words of Blith, "to make the poor rich, and the rich richer."[129]

Enclosure was also thought to be a solution to the constant conflict over use rights that threatened to disrupt the harmony of the countryside. Cressy Dymock made the point that lack of enclosure in England resulted in an "Inter-mixture of wayes and Interests," which he labeled "inconveniencies."[130] Because the land was held in common, a lack of clarity and precision in regard to who was to use it and how it was to be used led to disputes among the commoners over entitlement, to claims and counter-claims that caused perpetual antagonism and even disorder. Child was also anxious about the *"Inconveniencies"* arising from the conflicting claims to the use of waste land.[131] All of this recalls Locke's concern in chapter 7 with what he called "inconveniencies of the State of Nature." The purpose of civil society, he stated, was "to avoid, and remedy those inconveniencies of the State of Nature, which necessarily follow from every Man's being Judge in his own Case,"[132] by creating a known common authority that would resolve controversies of right, redress injuries, and prevent the commoners from resorting to violence. The troubles occurring over use rights in English wastes and commons and the remedy of enclosure proposed by the improvers, hence, may possibly have influenced Locke's perception of the difficulties in the state of nature and their termination by the establishment of civil government.

Whatever else it may be, chapter 5 is a significant argument for justifying enclosure in England. Beyond this, however, it is an ingenious rationale for colonialism, defending by implication the establishment of colonies and plantations in America and elsewhere and the enclosure and improvement of wastes in those wildernesses. Witness these words of Locke and all they suggest: "Yet there are still *great Tracts of Ground* to be found, which . . . *lie waste*, and are more than the People, who dwell on it, do, or can make use of, and so still lie in common."[133] Of some relevance in this connection is that the early eighteenth-century Scottish natural jurists, Gershom Carmichael and Francis Hutcheson, who highly esteemed the *Two Treatises*, used Locke's labor theory of property as the basis of a theory of occupation, a means of defining a rightful claim to previously unoccupied land like newly discovered overseas territories.[134]

Locke's thought decidedly reflected the productivity ideology of the improvers' brief for enclosure, and the self-interest of the landholder usually seems to have been a concern. The crucial passages are the following:

He who appropriates land to himself by his labour, does not lessen but increase the common stock of mankind. For the provisions serving to the support of humane life, produced by one acre of inclosed and cultivated land, are (to speak much within compasse) ten times more, than those, which are yeilded by an acre of Land, of an equal richnesse, lyeing wast in common. And therefor he, that incloses Land and has a greater plenty of the conveniencys of life from ten acres, than he could have from an hundred left to Nature, may truly be said, to give ninety acres to Mankind. For his labour now supplys him with provisions out of ten acres, which were but the product of an hundred lying in common. I have here rated the improved land very low in making its product but as ten to one, when it is much nearer an hundred to one.[135]

Nor is it so strange, as perhaps before consideration it may appear, that the *Property of labour* should be able to overballance the Community of Land. For 'tis *Labour* indeed that *puts the difference of value* on every thing; and let any one consider, what the difference is between an Acre of Land planted with Tobacco, or Sugar, sown with Wheat or Barley; and an Acre of the same Land lying in common, without any Husbandry upon it, and he will find, that the improvement of *labour makes* the far greater part of *the value*. I think it will be but a very modest Computation to say, that of the *Products* of the Earth useful to the Life of Man 9/10 are the *effects of labour*: nay, if we will rightly estimate things as they come to our use, and cast up the several Expences about them, what in them is purely owing to *Nature*, and what to *labour*, we shall find, that in most of them 99/100 are wholly to be put on the account of *labour*.[136]

For whatever *Bread* is more worth than Acorns, *Wine* than Water, and *Cloth* or *Silk* than Leaves, Skins, or Moss, that is wholly *owing to labour* and industry. The one of these being the Food and Rayment which unassisted Nature furnishes us with; the other provisions which our industry and pains prepare for us, which how much they exceed the other in value, when any one hath computed, he will then see, how much *labour makes the far greatest part of the value* of things, we enjoy in this World: And the ground which produces the materials, is scarce to be reckon'd in, as any, or at most, but a very small, part of it.[137]

An Acre of Land that bears here Twenty Bushels of Wheat, and another in *America*, which, with the same Husbandry, would do the like, are, without doubt, of the same natural, intrinsick Value. But yet the Benefit Mankind receives from the one, in a Year, is worth 5 l. and from the other possibly not worth a Penny, if all the Profit an *Indian* received from it were to be valued, and sold here; at least, I may truly say, not 1/1000. 'Tis *Labour* then which *puts the greatest part of Value upon Land*, without which it would scarcely be worth any thing: 'tis to that we owe the greatest part of all its useful Products: for all that the Straw, Bran, Bread, of that Acre of Wheat, is more worth than the Product of an Acre of as good Land, which lies wast, is all the Effect of Labour.[138]

Locke had apparently been enchanted by the ideas of Petty and by the improvers' alchemy of transmuting barren land into lucrative fertility.[139] Frequent ratios between the value of enclosed and unenclosed land appeared in the literature of the improvers and those influenced by them.[140] Gabriel Plattes, friend of Hartlib and one of the first important improvers, had estimated that unenclosed land was "not now yielding one-fourth part of that profit either to private or publique."[141] In his preface "To My Sons," Sir Richard Weston had said: "The Usurer doubles but his principall with Interest upon Interest in seven years, but by this little treatise you shall learn how to do more than treble your principall within the compass of one year."[142] The magic formula that he had devised from his experience in Brabant and Flanders was for making a profit of £7,800 in five years time by cultivating 500 acres of waste, planting it in rotation with flax, turnips, and oats undersown with clover.[143] The turnips and clover were to be used for livestock, thereby increasing their number and the output of manure, which in turn could be used to fertilize and increase the crops, in what E. J. Russell calls "an ascending spiral of productiveness."[144] By using clover and sainfoin, Houghton claimed, the value of an acre could be raised from two to thirty shillings,[145] and two years after enclosing, improving, and sowing them with oats and clover, eight acres of common field, originally letting for £3, were now bringing in nearly £40.[146] Three times as much livestock, according to Nehemiah Grew, could be supported on enclosed rather than open pasture,[147] and one acre of enclosed field would produce six times more food than an open field of equal size.[148] *The English Improver* of Walter Blith was subtitled: *Discovering to the Kingdome, That Some Land, Both Arrable and Pasture, May Be Advanced Double or Treble; Other Land to a Five or Tenfold: And Some to a Twenty Fold Improvement: Yea, Some Now Not Worth Above One, or Two Shillings, per Acree, Be Made Worth Thirty, or Forty, if not More.*[149] In his dedication to Parliament, Blith maintained that some tenants had doubled the value of their holdings by improvements and that he himself by watering his own land had increased the yield from six to twenty loads of hay.[150] Later in the work he made these estimates of increasing land values by enclosure: the "worst sort," by ten times; "midle sorts," by two; "richest Land," by three or four.[151] Again, he suggested that the relative profits of enclosed and unenclosed land were approximately in the ratio of three to one.[152] A dyer's crop like weld, which could be grown on worthless land without much attention, might increase its value by as much as sixteen times.[153] Yet Blith never was completely carried away by this agricultural magic to the extent that Ad. Speed was, whom he severely took to task for rashly promising increases up to 200 fold.[154] One of the questions on enclosure asked by Child was: "If that poor men might not imploy 2 Acres enclosed to more advantage; than twice as much in a *Common*?"[155] In similar vein Joseph Lee affirmed in 1654 that "the monarch of one acre will make more profit thereof, than he that hath his share in forty in common,"[156] a feeling repeated by a fellow preacher and distinguished wit, Thomas Fuller:

"The poor man who is monarch of but one enclosed acre will receive more profit from it than from his share of many acres in common with others."[157] In section 41 Locke explained that because of the lack of enclosure and improvement, the Americans "are rich in Land, and poor in all the Comforts of Life," and for this reason "a King of a large and fruitful Territory there feeds, lodges, and is clad worse than a day Labourer in *England*."[158] This was much the same contention of Edward Chamberlayne in *Angliae notitia* (1669), that "day labourers . . . by their large wages given them, and the cheapness of all necessaries, enjoy better dwellings, diet, and apparel in England than the husbandmen do in many other countries."[159]

Locke's recourse to the language of the agricultural improvers perhaps indicates the nature of his intended audience when he first composed chapter 5 during the Exclusion Crisis. In a recent essay,[160] Richard Ashcraft has convincingly argued that the *Second Treatise* was most probably written shortly after the dissolution of the Oxford Parliament in March 1681 to serve the political ends of the Whig conspiracy against Charles II being masterminded by Shaftesbury.[161] Maintaining that the political tract was "Janus-faced" with a conservative and a radical mien, Ashcraft focuses on the latter aspect because of its neglect by commentators.[162] Locke's work, Ashcraft demonstrates, shared in the radical political language and concepts common to a vast literature of Whig exclusion tracts and pamphlets written by lawyers, doctors, clerics, and journalists committed to the cause.[163] Their conceptual vocabulary was especially congenial to "the core and dynamic impetus" of the movement, the so-called "rabble" of small tradesmen and artisans, and old Commonwealth army officers.[164]

In contrast to Ashcraft's efforts, the preceding emphasis has been on the conservative component of the *Second Treatise*, the nucleus of which is chapter 5, a portion of the whole directed not so much to these radical "hotheads" as to "persons of quality," "good and sober" gentlemen, and their following among the yeomen.[165] For the Whigs, as Ashcraft recognizes, were basically a country party of landholders with a large radical element of townsmen, particularly in the City.[166] Ever the astute politician and sophisticated manipulator of symbols, Locke employed in chapter 5 the very discourse that would have been best understood and appreciated by a literate audience of Whig country gentlemen and farmers. Although Locke began the chapter with the radical language of equality, liberty, "Fellow-Commoners," a labor theory of property, natural right, and use production, his stress tends to shift to a more conservative vocabulary of landed property, property differentials, money, exchange production, wage labor, commerce, and it ends with improvement, the problem of waste, the advantages of enclosure, and agricultural productivity. It is this particular discourse that would have been far less meaningful and congenial to radical urban merchants and craftsmen than to progressive Whig husbandmen, a point suggested by Houghton's comment at the time that "most of our Nobility and Gentry are daily conversant about Improvements."[167]

Six years before the probable writing of the *Second Treatise*, the Whig pamphlet, *A Letter from a Person of Quality to His Friend in the Country* (1675) had been published anonymously,[168] then and long afterward credited to Locke's authorship, a judgment now generally discounted.[169] Of interest for our thesis is that the pamphlet concluded with a vehement rejection of the principle of divine right (used to cloak and justify royal absolutism) as a flagrant assault on the "properties, rights, and liberties" of Englishmen.[170] Divine right, the charge was made, violated "our Magna Charta."[171] In chapter 5 Locke was opposing precisely this use of divine right to legitimate the absolutism of Charles II in the later form of the Tory resurrection of Filmer's patriarchalism and its threat to the security of landed property. Taking the radical leveling slogan of liberty and equality against tyranny, Locke transformed it into a more conservative justification of inequality in landed property against absolutism, a position bound to have an irresistable appeal to Whig husbandmen of upper and middling rank.

If Locke originally intended chapter 5 for the "good and sober" Whig countrymen, subsequently he remained just as steadfast in his conviction about the crucial importance of the security and productivity of landed property and its relevance to politics. In the late nineties, after several exacting years in confronting concrete problems of domestic and colonial economic policy, Locke as a commissioner of the Board of Trade added the following passage to chapter 5:

This shews, how much numbers of men are to be preferd to largenesse of dominions, and that the increase of lands and the right imploying of them is the great art of government. And that Prince who shall be so wise and godlike as by established laws of liberty to secure protection and incouragement to the honest industry of Mankind against the oppression of power and narrownesse of Party will quickly be too hard for his neighbours.[172]

Petty had written long before that it was "a mistake, that the greatness and glory of a Prince lyeth rather in the extent of his Territory, then in the number, art, and industry of his people, well united and governed."[173]

Not only does there seem to be no significant contradiction between Locke's economic writings and chapter 5, but they also are mutually sustaining, each supplementing the other.

CHAPTER FIVE

Consideration of
an Opposing View

Because James Tully's position is almost diametrically opposed to the one just presented, and because he sees Locke's thought as antithetical to capitalism, serious attention must be given to his recently praised analysis. His aim is to locate the *Two Treatises*, especially chapter 5, in the realm of the natural law discourse of thinkers like Thomas, Suarez, Grotius, and Pufendorf, whose normative language was used by Locke to attack Filmer. Thus Tully hopes to "understand" Locke's "intentions" by replacing his "argument in its context" and thereby "to recover its original meaning."[1] The resulting treatment is certainly a novel one, disputing as it does the traditional "constitutionalist" approach to Locke and the more recent "bourgeois" interpretations of C. B. Macpherson and Leo Strauss. What follows, therefore, will be an attempt, at the risk of doing considerable injustice to an ingenious, compelling, and complex work of scholarship, to summarize some of the major aspects of Tully's thesis, and then to examine in more detail points relevant to what has been previously said about Locke and agrarian capitalism.

Locke's state of nature prior to the institution of money, according to Tully, is an egalitarian golden age of small-holders who are tenants in common under God. The holdings are conditional on their being used to satisfy the needs of the proprietor, providing they do not infringe on the needs of others. Men have an "inclusive" natural right, not an unconditional private right, to property. Property rights in the state of nature and in political society are always use rights. In nature and society each individual under the law of nature possesses an "exclusive" natural right to life, liberty, and possessions in the sense of self-preservation, the liberty consonant with preserving oneself and others, and the material possessions necessary for such preservation. The entitlement to all possessions is conditional on their use not simply for mere preservation but for the comfortable subsistance of the individual and his family. Only the products of the land in the state of nature are alienable, not the land itself. Labor is inalienable and wage labor is nonexistent. The quite different master-servant relationship, however, does occur. In contrast to wage labor, it entails the contracting of the free individual, unforced in any way, to perform a complete and unsupervised service for the master in exchange for payment in kind or service, in effect a kind of association for mutual aid. Exclusive right to possessions to be used for preservation is acquired through labor, inheritance, and charity. All men are duty-bound in nature and society by the first and fundamental law of nature—the preservation of society—to be charitable toward their less fortunate fellows, to ensure that they too have sufficient for their preservation, if circumstances should prevent their attaining that goal. The idyllic natural state of equality comes to an abrupt end with the introduction of money, preceded by barter. Money represents "the fall of man," and with it a great impulse is given to covetousness, arising out of barter. Both covetousness and its primary source, money, are condemned by Locke. The accumulation of more than an individual needs for his preservation, the acquisition of large holdings, and the appearance of widespread property differentials flow from the fount of all evil, money. Not productivity but money enables man to overcome the sufficiency limitation, in addition to that of spoilage. Increasing the productivity of a parcel of land through industry and improvement simply means that it should be unnecessary to extend the holding, and that more will be left to others.

Because of money, a growing covetousness, and the accompanying greed for land and possessions at the expense of others, conflicts arise in the state of nature. Political society and the coercive power of government then become imperative for the regulation of social relationships and to "bring the actions of men once again in line with God's intentions."[2] In creating and entering political society men surrender all their possessions to the community. Subsequently, all property is owned by the community, and individual holdings are defined by convention, by the civil law based on common consent. Landed property in political society is always a conventional, not a natural, right; it is inclusive, not exclusive. The natural right to property in the state of nature is not the foundation of property in political society. But like the right to property in nature, the right in political society is inclusive and dependent on use. Just as in nature, the member of political society does have the exclusive natural rights to life, liberty, and the possessions required for preservation. Any surplus above and beyond what is needed for the preservation of himself and family effectively belongs to the community. Each member has a responsibility toward all the others, a charitable duty. The family is a microcosm of the kind of human relationships that should in general characterize both the state of nature and political society. Locke's conception of the family, so opposed to Filmer's view, is nonpatriarchal and egalitarian, all children having an equal right in sharing the community of property. In thus attacking primogeniture, and in his objections to enclosure, Locke is advocating a much broader distribution of property than actually existed in England. The chief purpose of political society, subject to the moral precepts of natural law and communal consent based on universal male adult suffrage, is the public good, fundamental to which is the guarantee of the equal preservation of the life and liberty of all and the regulation of property as the means to that end. For Tully, "If there is one leitmotiv which unites Locke's works it is surely a philosophy of religious praxis."[3] The contribution made by the *Two Treatises* to this unifying theme is the vision of a self-governing political community embodying the egalitarianism of Levellers like John Lilburne and Richard Overton, one consisting of small and middling proprietors, all of whom will be able to live in security and relative comfort and enjoy the fruits of their callings.

An initial problem arises in attempting to reconcile Tully's provocative reading of the *Two Treatises* with our knowledge of Locke's social values gathered from his life and other writings. How does one balance Tully's Locke with the Locke who justified slavery and invested in the slave trade, approved of indentured servants and the apprentice system, charged interest on loans to close friends and was always tight-fisted and demanding in money transactions, recommended a most inhumane—even for his times—reform of the poor laws, and bequeathed only a minute proportion of a total cash legacy of over £12,000 to charity? This is also the Locke who took for granted without criticism the landed status quo and social hierarchy of England; directed much of his attention to the improvement of the gentry; saw nothing unjust in great disparities of income, wide property differentials, or in a majority of the population living at a bare subsistence level; and faithfully served the Whig aristocracy, many of whose inegalitarian social values were his own. These are facts neither noted nor explained away by Tully. Are we to assume, then, that the egalitarian social doctrine of the *Two Treatises* as explicated by Tully is an intellectual aberration that cannot be squared with our understanding of Locke as a whole, or is Tully's interpretation in error?

On the basis of what we know of Locke and his age, Tully's argument that Locke was a social and political egalitarian who shared in the leveling tendencies of Lilburne and Overton simply transcends the bounds of common sense and empirical evidence.[4] A fundamental and often unexpressed social assumption of Locke and his contemporaries was the distinction between gentlemen and non-gentlemen, rulers and ruled. This unquestioned article of faith in part accounted for the gentlemanly belief that the majority must always live "a hand to mouth" existence,[5] and it helps explain the contemptuous and abusive references of Locke and his peers to the lower classes, among them being: "the vulgar,"[6] "multitude,"[7] "herd,"[8] "rabble,"[9] "many-headed beast,"[10] "untamed beast,"[11] "begging drones,"[12] and "idle vagabonds."[13] According to Locke they were "as impatient of restraint as the sea,"[14] "always craving, never satisfied,"[15] "always superstitious and therefore empty-headed";[16] they did "reason but ill"[17] and were "destined to labour and given up to the service of their bellies."[18] Since the "greatest part cannot know, and therefore . . . must believe," Locke advised that giving them "plain commands, is the sure and the only course to bring them to obedience and practice."[19]

Some analysts of the history of political thought either gloss over this kind of ingrained upper-class prejudice or discount it as being of little relevance. On the one hand, they take for granted that Locke, even though he was not very specific on the matter, conformed to prevailing social attitudes and relegated women to a distinctly inferior status. On the other hand, commentators seem oddly reluctant, in the absence of any very explicit evidence to the contrary in the *Two*

Treatises, to take for granted his doing the same to the vast majority of his male compatriots, despite the fact that he would no less than in the case of women be subject to a predisposition typical of his station.

The outlook of Locke and his fellow gentlemen on the question of government and the status of the lower classes seems not very different from that of Sir Thomas Smith writing in the latter part of the previous century. Locke had most probably read Smith, although he evidently never owned *De republica anglorum*, and he recommended it for a summary knowledge of the English constitution.[20] The public-spirited Smith, a learned Cambridge scholar, laid out the structure of English society in a forthright way that few were to match. He constructed what we might label a primitive political sociology. Englishmen, he wrote, were divided into "foure sortes, gentlemen, citizens or burgesses, yeomen artificers, and laborers."[21] Gentlemen consisted of peers and gentry:

Whosoever studieth the lawes of the realme, who studieth in the universities, who professeth liberall sciences, and to be shorte, who can live idly and without manuall labour, and will beare the port, charge and countenaunce of a gentleman, he shall be called master, for that is the title which men give to esquires and other gentlemen, and shall be taken for a gentleman.[22]

Citizens and burgesses were those eligible for office in their cities and boroughs and who paid rates.[23] A yeoman was a forty-shilling freeholder and in addition as a tenant farmed the lands of gentlemen.[24] The last "sorte" included day laborers; poor husbandmen; and merchants, tradesmen, and artisans without free land.[25]

In his explanation of the constitutional system, Smith, a serious student of classical antiquity, thought it illuminating to compare ancient Rome with England. *Senatus populusque Romanus*, he reasoned, when translated into contemporary English reality, was the equivalent of lords and commons.[26] The commons like the *populus Romanus* consisted of "*equites* and *plebem*": "So when we in England do say the Lordes and the commons, the knights, esquires, and other gentlemen, with citizens, burgesses and yeomen be accompted to make the commons."[27] In the House of Lords sat the Lords Temporal and Spiritual, and in the House of Commons, knights, other gentlemen, citizens and burgesses. England was ruled by the monarch, gentlemen, citizens and burgesses, and yeomen. Although the last "sorte" did not themselves sit in the Commons, they had the vote and possessed other governmental duties.[28] The most numerous "sorte," the laborers and propertyless, were not meant to rule but only to be ruled by the minority made up of the other three classes.[29] Nevertheless, in a classic definition of virtual representation, Smith affirmed that in Parliament

> everie Englishman is intended to bee there present, either in person or by procuration and attornies, of what preheminence, state, dignitie, or qualitie soever he be, from the Prince (be he King or Queene) to the lowest person of Englande. And the consent of the Parliament is taken to be everie mans consent.[30]

This common understanding of English society and polity cannot be ignored, as Tully obviously has, in reading seventeenth-century authors like Locke.

Unquestionably, Locke was a sincere Christian, who like many others of the faith before and after him believed in the fundamental moral equality of man, but who also like them was able in all good conscience to condone gross social and political inequalities. Christians are not saints, nor should we expect them to be so. Their professions of brotherly love, kindness, and charity are often not commensurate with their actual conduct. Often they give to Christian doctrine a special interpretation that is used to rationalize what others among the faithful might judge to be iniquitous. Since Roman times the Church fathers had inveighed against covetousness, but this does not imply an opposition to amassing wealth. Locke's designation of money, gold, silver, diamonds, and objects employed in barter by the words "things" and "durable things," in contrast to "Goods," "good things," "useful things" for useful objects,[31] can hardly justify Tully's claim that by this usage Locke was evincing his "moral disapproval" of money, and so on.[32] Apart from the question of "thing" in reference to money being a conventional usage, "things" in section 50, contrary to Tully's general interpretation, seem to include useful possessions, and in section 90 of the *First Treatise* "Goods" apparently denotes money as well as useful objects. Moreover, in a passage quoted by Tully, the use of the expression "Natures Goods" to distinguish useful objects from money simply suggests that the latter might be called an "artificial good" or "good of convention."[33]

For a person who so disapproved of money—at least by Tully's account[34]—it is astounding that Locke allotted so much time and energy to accumulating it and to thinking and writing about it in such a positive way. Money for him was not so much an evil as something that could be used for good or evil purposes. While Locke apparently did not subscribe to the doctrine of original sin, he did hold that men were by nature selfish, partial to themselves, a quality not rooted in money but one that money might increase. Locke, of course, wished to eradicate covetousness and greed from young children, which he believed, in the passage cited by Tully from *Some Thoughts Concerning Education*, were natural to them.[35] Locke urged the inculcation of children at an early age with the all-important distinction between *meum* and *tuum*.[36] They should acquire a strong sense of private property and be able to respect what belongs to others. It should be emphasized that in his recommendations, Locke had no wish to eliminate desire from children or adults, only to canalize it toward constructive ends, for desire, he believed, was the motor of civilized life, the generator of all endeavor and industry.[37]

To a great extent, covetousness, defined as a desire to have more than one needs, is a matter of degree. Human needs differ, and to agree with Tully that Locke believed all men to have an exclusive natural right only to the possessions needed for life and liberty does not necessarily imply greater social equality. Needs vary according to one's station in life, or such was the conviction of Locke and his peers, and consequently the possessions of a day laborer satisfying his needs for subsistence and comfort would have been inadequate for a man of affairs.

Such also is the case with charity.[38] Most dedicated Christians of Locke's generation would have insisted that charity begins at home. Our own interest must be secured first, then we should calculate the amount of our donations in terms of the different objects of our charitable intentions. Charity to an indisposed laborer's spouse must be proportionate, not numerically equal to charity to an admiral's widow. This notion of proportionate equality dependent on social status was ingrained in the consciousness not only of gentlemen of the time but also of those of lesser rank.[39] Perhaps Locke's final word on charity, clearly revealing the limitations imposed by his social prejudices, was in his proposal for the reform of the poor laws,[40] a work to which Tully never refers. There Locke stated categorically that "every one must have meat, drink, clothing, and firing," adding that "the true and proper relief of the poor" "consists in finding work for them, and taking care they do not live like drones upon the labour of others."[41]

Nowhere, however, does a passion for transforming Locke into a social egalitarian lead Tully further astray than in the analysis of the philosopher's conception of the family. Tully is correct in giving great importance to the family because Locke's idea of it is directed at Filmer's patriarchalism and serves as a model for social relationships in nature and political society.[42] But in general he tends to misrepresent Locke's views on the subject. Tully maintains that Locke held a "nonpatriarchal conception of the family," conceived of as a "communal organisation with common property."[43] Because the property of the family head, Tully argues, is not exclusively his, the very foundation of individual property rights is undermined. The belief that all children of the family share equally in the inheritance— a position ascribed by Tully to Locke—"dismembers," "undercuts," "dissolves," and "undermines" primogeniture, the major legal foundation of large landed estates.[44] The egalitarian and communitarian characteristics of the family together with the attack on primogeniture were meant by Locke, according to Tully, to be a call for a much broader distribution of property.

Locke made more concessions to the patriarchal family than Tully is ready to admit.[45] The father was clearly assigned a superior role. Authority in the family was shared by husband and wife, a feature indicated by Locke's expression "parental power" as distinct from "paternal power." But he thought the two forms could be used interchangeably, and it may be suggestive that in the main "paternal power" was employed. The father did not have absolute and arbitrary power over other members of the family, his actions being limited by the law of nature. The wife had free possession of her own property defined in the matrimonial contract and, under certain circumstances, the right of divorce. Nevertheless, the power of the husband was paramount. In case of conflict between husband and wife, his will prevailed because of his superior ability and strength. When it came to the children, Locke also implied that the father's word was final. The father's superiority extended "to the things of their common Interest and Property."[46] Although the children had an equal right to inherit the possessions of their father, he might legitimately bestow them in proportion to their behavior, more to some than to others.[47] The estate was definitely the father's property, and "he may dispose or settle it as he pleases."[48] Finally, the father was the only member of the family who could have political rights or hold public office. Children were subject only to the authority of the parents and not, like them, to natural and civil law.

Far from demolishing primogeniture, Locke only maintained that it existed by the civil law of the land, not by the law of God or nature.[49] In doing so he was opposing Filmer's position that primogeniture existed by the command of God and nature and was the only legitimate means of transmitting political power and property beginning with Adam. Primogeniture for Locke was a licit mode of inheritance determined by the civil laws of some countries, by no means universal, however. All children had a "joynt Title" or "equal Title" to inherit their father's property, but this did not mean an entitlement to equal portions as Tully seems to imply.[50] The father could dispose of the property at will, subject of course to the civil law. If primogeniture was the law of the land, then the entailed property must go to the eldest son, the remainder distributed among the children as the father saw fit. Nowhere did Locke criticize primogeniture per se, nor did he ever disapprove of the English laws of inheritance.

From the supposed egalitarian community of the family, Tully moves on to that of political society, the family writ large. It seems evident that Locke never advocated an absolute and unconditional right of private property in land. To be in political society as distinct from the state of nature meant placing one's private possessions under the jurisdiction of government. Property rights were established by convention, by the civil laws or "positive constitutions" of states, within, of course, the moral limits of the law of nature. In regard to the status of private property vis-à-vis government, Locke used such words as "settled," "regulate," "submit," "subject."[51] Governments defined property titles, set the laws of inheritance, distinguished private from common land, imposed taxes, resolved property disputes, stipulated methods of enclosure, controlled land use, and so on. However, in contending with Macpherson's idea that a market society entails a conception of precisely defined private property, Tully argues that Locke had in mind "community ownership of all possessions."[52] It "is the logical consequence of the premisses of Locke's theory in the *Two Treatises*."[53] Locke's notion of property in political society was, therefore, by Tully's reading, hardly compatible with the conditions conducive to capitalism. As evidence for Locke's supposed "community of property," Tully relies primarily on a single passage in the *Second Treatise*:

> Every Man, when he, at first, incorporates himself into any Commonwealth, he, by his uniting himself thereunto, annexed also, and submits to the Community those Possessions, which he has, or shall acquire, that do not already belong to any other Government. For it would be a direct Contradiction, for any one, to enter into Society with others for the securing and regulating of Property: And yet to suppose his Land, whose Property is to be regulated by the Laws of the Society, should be exempt from the Jurisdiction of that Government, to which he himself the Proprietor of the Land, is a Subject. By the same Act therefore, whereby any one unites his Person, which was before free, to any Commonwealth; by the same he unites his Possessions, which were before free, to it also; and they become, both of them, Person and Possession, subject to the Government and Dominion of that Commonwealth, as long as it hath a being. *Whoever* therefore, from thenceforth, by Inheritance, Purchase, Permission, or otherways *enjoys any part of the Land*, so annext to, and under the Government *of that Commonwealth, must take it with the Condition* it is under; that is, *of submitting to the Government of the Commonwealth*, under whose Jurisdiction it is, as far forth, as any Subject of it.[54]

With the possible exception of the two phrases "belong to any other Government" and "unites his possessions," Locke's language is similar to that of the previous passages cited above in which he employed "settled," "regulate," "submit," "subject" to describe the status of one's property, on entering political society, in relationship to government and the community as a whole. Had he intended "community ownership" of landed property, nothing said here or elsewhere confirms it. He seems to have been thinking of existing circumstances in England. In his writings he certainly distinguished between private and common land, between landlord and tenant, between the propertied and propertyless. If indeed all he had in mind by these distinctions was a difference in usufruct, then no explanation is forthcoming. But even if Locke had gone so far, as Tully contends, as to postulate community ownership of all land, it would make little difference from the standpoint of agrarian capitalist development as long as the use rights were clearly defined and subject to the rule of law. For the agrarian capitalist was primarily the tenant who used the fundamental means of production in land owned by others and who relied on the judicial process to protect his holding.

Tully's treatment of Locke's view of enclosure, which is at odds with my own, also illustrates his doubtful interpretation of the thinker's position on land ownership.[55] Tully thinks Locke was opposed to enforced enclosure by Parliamentary Act, citing as examples the defeated Bills of 1661, 1664, and 1681 that were sponsored by wealthy proprietors and would have legalized enclosure without consent. The sole evidence given by Tully for Locke's probable attitude toward enclosure is section 35 of the *Second Treatise*. In 34 Locke explained that God had given the world to men in common to be used for their benefit. In doing so God did not believe that it would always be common and uncultivated. In other words, God clearly intended his gift in common to be individuated by private appropriation and improved. The earth was given specifically to the use of the industrious and rational, and their labor was their title to it. Express consent of the other commoners was not necessary for individual appropriation, and no one should complain as long as he was left land as good as that which was appropriated and enclosed. But Locke saw a problem, for he began 35 with "'Tis true," and proceeded to acknowledge that circumstances differed in England and other civilized nations where commons existed by civil law and where therefore the consent of the commoners was required for any private appropriation and enclosure of common land. In such cases, the law must be upheld, or presumably changed according to the appropriate procedures. Locke was simply giving an example of historical fact, a description of a particular situation in existing political societies of an advanced kind in respect to the enclosure of commons determined by positive law, a condition quite different from the state of nature. Section 35 is not a moral argument against enclosure, as Tully seems to assume. It is only a parenthetical statement sandwiched between arguments about private appropriation, labor, industry, productivity, the virtue of improving waste land, the unimproved wilderness of America, and so on. Even if it can be conclusively demonstrated that Locke was against enforced enclosure, nothing he said or implied would justify Tully's conclusion that his "theory serves explicitly to legitimate the rights of the commoners against the enclosing landlords."[56]

A further example of Tully's idiosyncratic textual exegesis, singularly lacking in historical sensitivity, is related to the questions of appropriation, enclosure, and productivity. He takes issue with Macpherson's interpretation of section 37 of the *Second Treatise*.[57] The passage in question is: "He who appropriates land to himself by his labour, does not lessen but increase the common stock of mankind," because, by enclosing and improving ten acres, he could produce far more than one hundred "left to Nature" and consequently "may truly be said to give ninety acres to Mankind." According to Tully this means that the increase of the productivity of an allotment in the state of nature by the labor of the holder will render further appropriation unnecessary, and hence more land will be available for the use of others. Macpherson reads the passage to mean that "the greater productivity of the appropriated land more than makes up for the lack of land available for others."[58] Nothing said by Locke in sections 36 or 37, contrary to Tully's own assertion, seems decisively to support his reading as against Macpherson's. Because of the ambiguity of Locke's thoughts on the matter, however, the correctness of Macpherson's reading can be demonstrated by reference to the contexts of the improver's discourse and English social history.

First, with few exceptions, the improvers believed that the larger the holding the greater its productivity. Far from being based on mere conjecture, this judgment rested on what appeared to be true of actual agrarian practice. Locke's unremitting emphasis on productivity and his use of the language of the improvers suggests that he accepted both the principle and the practice. In referring to numbers being more relevant to productivity than actual acreage, he, like the improvers, was thinking more of countries or "nations"—little England in contrast to vast America—than of individual holdings.

Second, the improvers stressed how enclosure and the resulting increase in productivity would not only mean greater profits for the encloser but would also benefit mankind in terms of more commodities to be distributed and more employment opportunities for the poor. On the basis of this kind of argument a few even prescribed enforced enclosure. In a strictly limited and relative sense there was an element of truth to the claims of the improvers. From the standpoint of the actual agricultural situation in England, food was in abundance and prices were low, so that the worker was better fed and clothed than elsewhere, at least according to contemporary accounts.

In further pressing his egalitarian thesis, Tully makes the following statement:

The conventional criterion for the right to vote in the seventeenth century was the possession of property. Filmer's theory systematically denies property, and therefore suffrage, to all but independent landholders. In demonstrating that every man has property in his life, liberty, person, action and some possessions, Locke extends the franchise to every adult male. He does not explicitly state the criterion in the *Two Treatises*; he simply assumes it as the basis of his discussion of various kinds of representation: "whenever the People shall chuse their *Representatives upon* just and undeniably *equal measures* suitable to the original Frame of Government, it cannot be doubted to be the will and act of the Society" (2.158). The equal measures suitable to the original constitution cannot but be the natural equality of all men (2.5). Locke's theory thus serves to justify the Exclusion strategy of the Whigs to make representation as broadly based as possible (Dunn 1969, pp. 44–57; Plumb 1967, pp. 31–65).[59]

What Locke apparently intended by the "original Frame of Government," on the basis of this and the equally important preceding section 157, was the mode of representation before the recent corruption and decay of the system. "*Equal measures*," far from signifying the "natural equality of all men," seems to refer to a uniformity of franchise in place of the peculiar mixture and variety of franchises that had developed. Finally, the two authorities cited, John Dunn and J. H. Plumb, simply do not support Tully's contentions about Locke.

Locke may have been saying three things in these two somewhat confusing sections, none of which seems to bear out Tully's interpretation and conclusion.[60] First, representation should be "in proportion to the assistance" that any part of the People "affords to the publick," which when read in conjunction with section 140 suggests that those who pay taxes should have the suffrage. Second, new corporations hitherto unrepresented should be granted the franchise. Third, old corporations, rotten boroughs whose population had dwindled, should be deprived of their representation.

Locke's outlook on these points must be placed in some kind of historical perspective, if it is to be grasped.[61] By the time of the English Revolution the franchise had definitely broadened. Of the adult male population, because of the efforts of the Long Parliament in its early months, between 27 and 40 percent were eligible to vote. After the Revolution the outlook of the gentry had hardened toward widening the franchise, which gradually became more restricted. During the Exclusion Crisis the Whig attitude was to use a broadened franchise to resist the encroaching power of the Crown. The word "representation" was first commonly used with a political meaning in 1679, the year of the unsuccessful Whig bill to reform the franchise. It called for a considerable restriction on the old forty-shilling freeholders, limiting the county vote to people with estates of at least a value of £200. The borough franchise was to be standardized, making them all "scot and lot," those householders of one year residence paying rates and owing service to borough courts, not necessarily a more democratic arrangement than the freeman and burgage franchises. An exception to this principle was to be the largest cities with freeman franchises: London, York, Bristol, Norwich, and Exeter. In London, the 4,000 liverymen entitled to vote were fewer in number than the total of freemen. In York, the electorate was about 75 percent of the adult male population, and in the three other cities about 50 percent. A document thought to be Shaftesbury's own proposals for the franchise sometime during the period recommended abolition of the borough anomalies and the adoption of a uniform franchise, a reform of the forty-shilling freehold requirement to correspond to the current equivalent in value, and very high property and age qualifications for all M.P.s. From the very complex and far from clear picture of the Whig position that emerges, it seems that in general they did wish to extend the franchise, only, however, in a very special sense. Rather than "to make representation as broadly based as possible," as Tully asserts, they wished in the main to extend suffrage horizontally and not vertically, that is, to include more people in the categories already represented, who were still disenfranchised, but not to extend it appreciably downward to include categories unrepresented. One important exception, however, to the horizontal extension was the raising of the forty-shilling freehold qualification for county voters, which would have meant a *reduction* of the former number of electors. Nothing said by Locke would indicate that he would go beyond any of this.

Finally, in a category distinct from the previous ones that have been criticized, and by far the most important and relevant to my thesis, is Tully's argument that Locke had no conception of the alienability of labor and that the master-servant relationship, as Locke described it, was far different from the nexus of capitalist and wage-laborer.[62] Because of this, Tully reasons, Locke's political thought must be totally dissociated from capitalism. The line of reasoning employed by Tully can be represented by the following. Since every man has property, he alone has a right to it. "Person" means to Locke a rational agent "capable of law."[63] It is the moral being of the individual, that which gives him identity in the form of the self-consciousness central to his thought and action. Just as one cannot alienate his person, so he cannot exchange or transfer the ownership of his labor, which is a part, an extension of his person through the instrument of his hands and body. For Locke, then, insists Tully, "it's logically impossible for an agent to alienate *his* labour."[64] Locke's model for labor and the laborer is *homo faber*, the creative or fabricating man, made by God, *deus faber*, in his own image. Labor, therefore, is the source of man's humanity, his divine and sacred quality. Man was conceived of by Locke in the image of the *dēmiourgos* or craftsman who mixed his labor with the raw, unshaped stuff of nature, imprinting it with a form and producing a complete work of art such as a table or shoes, one that combined "conception" and "execution." The laborer can legitimately exchange the object of his skill for some kind of payment. The finished product, table or shoes, thus becomes the property of the buyer, but not the labor of the craftsman.

How then does Tully explain the famous turfs passage of chapter 5: "Thus the Grass my Horse has bit; the Turfs my Servant has cut; and the Ore I have digg'd in any place where I have a right to them in common with others, become my *Property*."?[65] From Tully's standpoint Locke here was thinking not of a wage laborer, who exchanged his labor power as a commodity for wages, but of a servant as *homo faber* who performed an entire task and was paid by his master for that service. This is the essence of the master-servant relationship for Locke throughout the *Two Treatises*, Tully argues, and not the wage-relationship. Locke was consequently able to maintain intact his principle of the inalienability of labor without compromise or contradiction.

Several problems arise from this reading of Locke. Why, if Tully is correct, did Locke never explicitly deny the alienability of labor? Even though he was adamant about the inviolability and inalienability of one's person, he admitted that an individual who could not voluntarily surrender his life to another could under certain circumstances "forfeit" his freedom and be legitimately enslaved,[66] and he apparently accepted without protest the widespread institution of indenture.[67] Moreover, one's moral being, his person, seems to be conceptually different from his labor. One cannot give up his person without surrendering his life, but is this equally true of his labor?

The really critical issue, however, raised by Tully has to do with the distinction he makes between selling a service and alienating labor. His treatment of this point suggests that he fundamentally misunderstands the nature of wage labor and the sale of labor power. The traditional independent craftsman fashions a product like shoes or performs a specialized service, which he sells at a price. He may, of course, decide not to sell the shoes. The buyer purchases the commodity produced by the craftsman, not the labor power, even when the commodity is custom-made for the buyer. The craftsman may manufacture other shoes during the same time period, but they do not belong to our buyer, unless he is willing to pay for them and the craftsman wishes to sell them. In marked contrast to this craftsman, the wage laborer sells his labor power, instead of a product, in the form of labor time to his employer. Since the employee is selling his labor power, all that he produces in the time stipulated by the work contract is the property of the employer. The wage laborer has no claim to any products that he makes during the specified period of employment. All are owned by the employer. The unity of "conception" and "execution," stressed by Tully as the major characteristic of the function of the craftsman as against that of the wage laborer, is beside the point. A craftsman performing a complete service like making a pair of shoes can be a wage laborer. His labor power is exchanged for wages, and all the shoes made during the workday belong to the employer. This was actually the case with early capitalist factories, which were collections of artisans under one roof.

In the turfs passage Locke has returned from discussing the state of nature to a brief consideration of the commons of contemporary England.[68] His references elsewhere in the *Second Treatise* to the master-servant relationship make it clear that by "servant" in those sections he probably had in mind the "living-in servant," either in husbandry or the domestic. But we should not assume from this usage that he was doing likewise in the turfs passage. In addition to the specific meaning, *servant* was also customarily employed in England in a generic sense to designate any kind of laborer. A seventeenth-century author might often in the same volume vary the senses from page to page in which he used the term: in one instance, narrow, in another, broad. Locke in the passage evidently was not thinking of the task worker, since he never mentioned such agricultural laborers in his economic writings or in the *Two Treatises*. Much more likely, the servant is the day laborer paid a daily wage for the seasonal work of cutting the turfs. But whether "servant" in the context denotes "servant in husbandry" or day laborer really makes no fundamental difference. Both categories would receive wages for their labor.[69] It is important, however, that for Locke the servant in question represented a juridically free man who was being paid for his time, so that all he mixed his labor with—the turfs he cut—belonged to the employer according to their contractual agreement. Juridical freedom and the sale of labor power are the crux of the wage-labor relationship so essential to capitalism. Although Locke in chapter 5 resorted to an ancient mode of description, that is, "master" and "servant," that traditional mode was informed by the new conception of the alienability of labor that was articulated less ambiguously in the economic writings of 1668 and 1692. K. I. Vaughan never doubts that Locke had in mind the alienability of labor. Her comment on the turfs passage is worth quoting in full:

Clearly, then, ones labor can also include the product of the effort of someone one has hired, the wage serving as a proxy for acquiring title to the result. Already there is implied a two-part division under the general category of labor, the employer and the employee, the one who directs the operation and the one who follows directions. In addition, Locke has a third category which he includes under the name of labor, which is already implied in the "grass my horse has bit." Insofar as the horse is an instrument of production, it constitutes capital, and the product of its services belongs to its owner.[70]

Further treatment of the master-servant relationship by Tully is likewise characterized by serious shortcomings. Believing that the master-servant relationship existed in the state of nature as well as in political society, Locke described it in this way: "A Free-man makes himself a Servant to another, by selling him for a certain time, the Service he undertakes to do, in exchange for Wages he is to receive: And though this commonly puts him into the Family of his Master, and under the ordinary Discipline thereof; yet it gives the Master but a Temporary Power over him, and no greater, than what is contained in the *Contract* between 'em."[71] The master does not have arbitrary and absolute power over the servant as he legitimately would have over a slave. Tully comments on the passage thus:

Since it is a freeman who makes himself a servant, the agreement must presuppose that the choice not to become a servant is available to him. This condition is fulfilled by the availability of spontaneous products of nature and utilisable land on the English Common in the "turfs" passage. If, for some reason, there is no alternative, then the man is not free and the master-servant relation cannot arise. Locke is particularly emphatic on this point in his discussion of the right of the needy to support by charity.[72]

The *First Treatise* is then quoted by Tully to substantiate his last point: "Man can no more justly make use of another's necessity, to force him to become his Vassal, by with-holding that Relief, God requires him to afford to the wants of his Brother, than he that has more strength can seize upon a weaker, master him to his Obedience, and with a Dagger at his Throat offer him Death or Slavery."[73] Tully concludes: "This remarkable condition makes it impossible for the capitalist to appear in Locke's theory. If a man is driven by necessity to work for another, then the relation is based on force and is, *ipso facto*, a master and vassal arrangement. A person is not allowed to treat another in this way; he must feed him instead."[74]

This misreading of the definition of the master-servant relationship is very perplexing, indeed. When used by Locke in this context, "Free-man" was intended merely to denote the juridical status of the individual, to indicate that he was under no legal encumbrances to another. He is neither a child subject to his parents nor a vassal or slave bound to his lord. But that he was under no such obligations of the divine, natural, or civil law does not mean that he was completely "uncoerced," for example, by the necessity of working for another in order to survive. The lack of an alternative to employment as a servant, therefore, has nothing to do with the specification of "Free-man" in this sense. According to Tully's misinterpretation of Locke's meaning, why would anyone become a servant in the first place if he were not forced by circumstances to seek such service for the sake of a livelihood? Does he become a servant out of the kindness of his heart? Is it an act of charity or brotherly love? Locke supplied the answer in the section of the *First Treatise* immediately following the one from which Tully quotes, but to which he does not refer: "The Authority of the Rich Proprietor, and the Subjection of the Needy Beggar began not from the Possession of the Lord, but the Consent of the poor Man, who preferr'd being his Subject to starving. And the Man he thus submits to, can pretend to no more Power over him, than he has consented to, upon Compact."[75] The freeman, hence, is forced to become a servant to keep himself from starving. It is a voluntary act in that a gun is not pointed at him, forcing him to do so. He is free to seek employment elsewhere. The very essence of the wage relationship is precisely the juridically free status of the worker, so different from other juridically restricted conditions of economic dependence, such as those of vassal or slave. It is a nonhereditary, nonproprietary relationship, one that is voluntary and contractually limited and can be terminated by either party.

Tully, however, identifies the condition of the wage laborer under capitalism with the servitude of the slave or vassal who is physically forced to labor under the minute supervision and regulation of an absolute lord. Locke's servant, for Tully, as we have seen, is not a wage laborer but a maker analogous to God, *deus faber*, who sells a complete service combining both "conception" and "execution." The variety of workers in precapitalist society, each performing skilled and complete services, such as weaving, carpentry, shoemaking, is called the "social division of labour" by Tully. This precapitalist social division of labor, Tully asserts, is replaced by a new capitalist division of labor. Under capitalism the labor process is fragmented, as in the case of a typical factory, into many different and partial operations, each being performed by an individual worker, and conception is divorced from execution. The wage laborer, by performing a single fragmented function in the production of the whole commodity under the strictest direction of the capitalist, loses his humanity and is transformed from being a freeman into a vassal or slave. So different is the wage-laborer under capitalism, Tully contends, from Locke's servant that "it is incorrect and anachronistic to impute the assumption of capitalist wage-labour to Locke."[76]

Again, Tully's position raises important questions not only about the adequacy of his interpretation of Locke but also about the validity of his conception of capitalism itself, and its relationship to Locke. To begin with, Tully erroneously restricts the "social division of labour" to precapitalist society alone.[77] The opposition that concerns the authority on whom Tully relies—Harry Braverman, following Marx—is not between the social division of labor and the capitalist division of labor, as describing two different modes of the organization of work, but on the contrary is the social division of labor, referring to the division of labor within society generally, versus the division of labor within the individual workshop, that is, the "manufacturing" or "technical" division of labor.[78] Braverman, in fact, distinguishes quite precisely between the "social division of labour" and the "manufacturing division of labour." His chapter 3, entitled "The Division of Labour," is devoted to the manufacturing division of labor, which he calls the "earliest innovative principle of the capitalist mode of production."[79]

Contrary to Tully's misconception, the social division of labor exists in every society, precapitalist and capitalist, and has to do with the division of function and skills. On the other hand, the manufacturing division of labor is concerned with the fragmentation of the labor process within a single industrial enterprise that may occur in precapitalist societies but that develops in an extreme and universal form under capitalism. Braverman states categorically—a vital point ignored by Tully—that the manufacturing division of labor so central to the labor process under mature capitalism develops and spreads only very slowly in the early stages: "At first, the capitalist utilizes labor as it comes to him from prior forms of production, carrying on labor processes as they had been carried on before. . . . These early workshops were simply agglomerations of smaller units of production, reflecting little change in traditional methods, and the work thus remained under the immediate control of the producers in whom was embodied the traditional knowledge and skills of their crafts."[80] Typical of immature capitalism in the transitional period was subcontracting, "putting-out" systems, and cottage industry.[81] Only much later were the technical processes of capitalist production revolutionized and universalized. Marx himself clearly differentiated primitive from fully developed industrial capitalism in much the same terms, by introducing the notions of the "formal" and "real subjection" of labor to capital.[82] The early stages feature only a formal subjection as the artisan becomes a wage laborer. A more advanced capitalism, in contrast, is characterized by a real subjection rendered possible through the technical transformation of the traditional labor process. Marx never identified capitalist wage labor, as Tully does, with slavery or vassalage (except metaphorically, as with "wage-slavery"), for to do so would be to obscure the very essence of wage labor: its juridically free status. This, together with the separation of the worker from the means of production, is the condition of economic exploitation by means of the extraction of surplus value, as distinct from "extra-economic" modes of exploitation.[83]

All of this has a direct bearing on the validity of the logic of Tully's argument against Locke as a "capitalist theorist." Since Locke's ideas failed to reflect adequately the form and values of advanced industrial capitalism, he had no connection whatsoever with capitalism, or so Tully mistakenly assumes. Obviously, no one, least of all Macpherson, would be so naive as to argue that Locke was a James Ramsay McCulloch. In other words, a fundamental shortcoming of Tully's analysis is a failure to perceive capitalism as an historical phenomenon, developing over the centuries from bare beginnings to a complex and mature stage. Classic British capitalism of the nineteenth century and the social relations of production it entailed did not suddenly spring forth full-blown at that time but had their roots in the soil of Locke's England. What we should be searching for in his ideas, among other things, is some discernible sign of those roots beginning to shoot, not some miraculous premonition of the end-result. At best we can maintain that Locke's thought was in part expressive of certain basic social changes occurring in England, of a transition to the early stages of capitalism, and that he began to conceive of the social relations of production in a manner suggestive of an embryonic capitalist outlook. One might argue that some of Locke's ideas symbolize or represent the "formal" subjection of labor to capital, and perhaps the beginnings of the "real" subjection. The argument here has been that Locke's thought testified to important changes in agriculture and the social relations of agricultural production, the necessary conditions for the eventual emergence of English industrial capitalism. Agrarian capitalism and its telling social effects on the English countryside, which may be so relevant to an understanding of Locke's political theory, however, are beyond Tully's ken. Like many others, he is the prisoner, albeit a protesting one, of the fashionable stereotype of Locke, the bourgeois ideologist of mercantile and manufacturing capitalism. Thus, much of Tully's attack, whatever its imperfections, is against a straw man.

CHAPTER SIX

The Unity of
Locke's Thought

If analysis of Locke's economic writings and chapter 5 of the *Second Treatise* within the context of English social history reveals a theory of early agrarian capitalism, what is the relationship of these writings to the totality of his thought, in particular to the whole of the *Second Treatise* and to the philosophy of *An Essay Concerning Human Understanding*? Scholars commonly view Locke as essentially a pluralistic thinker, and they consider each aspect of his thought—for example, the philosophical, political, and economic—to be more or less self-contained and segregated, with little mutual connection between them. No close logical relationship is judged to exist between the political thought of the *Two Treatises* and the philosophic doctrines of the *Essay* similar to that which is seen between parts 1 and 2 of Hobbes's *Leviathan*. Locke, according to this interpretation, simply failed to construct an all-embracing and integrated structure of philosophical, political, and economic ideas, in contrast to some great philosophers from Plato to Hegel. No one could sensibly dispute this assessment, but agreement with it does not necessarily entail acceptance of the position that Locke's thought is characterized by a number of separate parts without any common unifying and informing themes or problems. Locke's thought, in actuality, can be perceived as constituting a whole, although the elements are not mutually related in any rigorous logical fashion. One of the virtues of the argument so far advanced is that it may suggest something about the nature of this unity.

From the methodological standpoint, it has been previously argued that both the economic memorandum of 1668 and chapter 5 are examples of the application of the mode of Baconian natural history to social analysis. Locke's social thought, consequently, is seen from a previously unrecognized perspective. A partial answer, moreover, has been found to the question of the unity of his social and philosophic ideas, since the *Essay* is also a work of Baconian inspiration, although few twentieth-century scholars, with the important exceptions of Fulton Anderson and John Yolton, have acknowledged the fact.[1] The lord chancellor's influence is testified to by the title, form, and style of the book; by the author's awareness of the novelty of his endeavor; and by his emphasis on intellectual cooperation, dedication to the quest for truth, disparagement of schoolmen, concern with usefulness, and conviction in the conformity of his doctrine to Christian belief.[2] Of more significance, however, is Locke's indebtedness to Verulam's famous conception of the "idols," and above all to his mode of natural history with its premium on experience, experiment, and practical utility. In short, the *Essay* is a Baconian natural history of the understanding, doing for the psyche what Boyle, Sydenham, and Hooke had already accomplished in their pioneer efforts in the fields of chemistry, medicine, and microscopy. A definite intellectual link, therefore, has been identified as joining three apparently disparate works in the corpus of Locke's writings.

Baconian natural history applied to the study of society in the seventeenth century, however, was not simply a matter of method. A substantive bond of Baconian origin also places the memorandum of 1668 and chapter 5 in juxtaposition even if not forging a further link between them and the *Essay*.[3] The common denominator of the two earlier works is the attention given to agricultural property and its use and organization, a theme typical of the tracts of the Baconian improvers. The memorandum suggested the triadic structure of the agrarian sector and the conception of the day laborer as the juridically free man separated from the means of production whose labor power was a commodity to be exchanged for wages in the market. These ideas were rendered more explicit and expanded in the published version of 1692. Chapter 5 focused on other matters of a closely related nature, also dear to the Baconian agrarian reformers: common and waste land, appropriation and enclosure, agricultural improvement and productivity, labor and population. Far from being at variance with the technical economic analyses of 1668 and 1692, the ideas of chapter 5 were ancillary and supplemental to them. Together, they are of a piece and offer compelling evidence for terming Locke a theorist of early agrarian capitalism.

Baconianism aside, however, can the *Second Treatise* as a whole and the later works—the *Essay* and *Some Thoughts Concerning Education*—feasibly be related to the thesis about Locke and agrarian capitalism? To begin with the *Second Treatise*, only chapter 5 dealt with agriculture and problems of productivity. Nevertheless, the book throughout was concerned with questions of landed property, property rights, and conflicts of interest arising from property. The primary purpose of government, Locke stressed, was to secure and protect not only the lives and liberties of citizens but also their properties. Political society, indeed, was first established for this very reason, to settle on a commonly recognized body of rules to regulate human conduct, a judge to interpret and apply those rules, and the power at his disposal to enforce his decisions. Only thus would the controversies over land holdings in the state of nature—those "inconveniencies" as Locke and the agrarian improvers called them—be resolved fairly without violence and bloodshed. Political society, then, was instituted in order to prevent the state of nature from becoming a state of war among individuals and factions largely contending over their landed properties.

Locke's conception of the state seems to have been based on a juridical model, the idea of a judge who arbitrated in the disputes between parties under his authority.[4] For this reason Locke was fond of calling government an "Umpire," a common legal term for an arbitrator.[5] Of course, in seventeenth-century England, among the major contentions settled by the judiciary in particular and government in general were those having to do with property rights, as one might expect especially with landed property: disputes over titles, boundaries, encroachment, enclosure, inheritance, and so on. These, of course, were matters that deeply interested and directly affected the Whig magnates whom Locke served. Furthermore, by locating the supreme sovereign or rule-making power in the king in Parliament, subject only to the approval of the community of landholders, Locke assured that the peers and gentry were firmly in control.

A realist with a shrewd, practical political eye, Locke always gave priority to the necessity of coercive sanctions, the most indispensable being the death penalty, as the basis of political power and civil law.[6] The commonwealth he recommended in the *Second Treatise* was a system of interest ultimately held together by the consensus of the landed classes. When, however, the clash of narrow and divergent interests threatened the preservation of the common welfare and civil order, the coercive power at the disposal of government ensured unity and stability. Locke, consequently, in the *Second Treatise* prescribed a hierarchical structure of power that would be most conducive to Whig interests and at the same time would contain any centrifugal tendencies generated by those interests. Nor should it be forgotten that Whig landholders in the south and east were in the forefront of the development of agrarian capitalism. Perhaps the "Industrious and Rational" of chapter 5, those enterprising and productive appropriators who were the true inheritors of the land originally bequeathed by God to mankind in common, were cast by Locke in the image of these same innovative Whig agriculturalists.[7]

Concerned as it was with the psyche and saying nothing about landed property or agriculture, how then did Locke's other Baconian natural history, the *Essay*, fit into the scheme? Since the "Industrious and Rational" landholders of chapter 5 were the real beneficiaries of God's gift to man, one might surmise that somewhere in Locke's writings he would delineate their nature. This seems to be precisely the case with the *Essay*. What better place than in a book devoted to an inquiry into knowledge and the understanding to give some attention to the subject?[8] This would be a doubly suitable place, moreover, because Locke never thought of the work as a technical treatise written for specialists. He intended that it should be read by a broad spectrum of ordinary, educated readers: gentry, merchants and businessmen, clergy, lawyers, doctors, and men of letters. Among other purposes he meant it to be a kind of practical manual for the orientation and guidance of his audience in their day-to-day affairs as well as in their "great Concernments" of religion, morality, law, and politics. Not that the *Essay* offered any detailed or exact prescriptions for conduct, but it did aim at making men self-conscious about their mental processes, the assumptions of their thought and action, and the grounds of those assumptions and their validity. Aids to assessing the truth or falsehood of propositions and arguments were provided by Locke to his readers. In addition, in all that he said about these subjects, Locke succeeded in conveying a model or ideal of the rational individual, of what it would be like in varying circumstances to act in a rational fashion.

Locke, in most of what he wrote in his later years, seems to have believed that he had a special calling to educate his fellow countrymen, to reform and revitalize them by changing their attitude to life and the way they acted. The *Essay* belonged to the same genre of didactic works as Bacon's *Instauratio magna*, but Locke's purpose was considerably more modest than that of the lord chancellor. Locke's aim was to launch a much less ambitious instauration: to suggest how men might act in a more rational way than they had in the past. Over the years he had become increasingly perturbed by what he took to be the decline of the gentry. He criticized them, as we have seen, for their slothful and extravagant living. They were idle, he believed, given to expensive vanity and self-indulgence, to spending beyond their means only for the present with little thought of the future. They lacked industry, frugality, and sobriety, mismanaging their estates with the result that many became bankrupt. Locke apparently thought of his role as that of changing for the better these corrupt but critical actors in English society by showing them how to become more industrious and rational individuals. He wished, on the one hand, to rejuvenate the gentry. On the other hand, he was distressed by what he took to be the laziness and profligacy of the vast mass of the lower classes, and hence he was deeply concerned with improving labor discipline, transforming the impoverished, propertyless majority into an industrious, thrifty, God-fearing, and compliant work force. Most of his energies were expended on the former task, but his seldom-read memorandum of 1697 on the reform of the poor laws is an obvious example of his worry over the latter problem.

Evidently Locke thought that the question of the country gentlemen was especially vital, not only because they were the proprietors of the landed estates that fed, clothed, and housed all Englishmen but also because they were the backbone of law and order in the rural society where the overwhelming number of the populace lived. Moreover, isolated as many of the gentry were in the countryside, their intellectual horizons were prone to be limited and their understandings severely restricted. They were too frequently far removed in spirit and outlook from the original industrious and rational cultivators and improvers of God's earth. If England were to safeguard and strengthen its position in a hostile world, then the gentry, the very foundation of society, polity, and economy, must renounce their irrational mode of conduct. Locke suffered from no illusions about the country squire

who, leaving Latin and learning in the university, removes thence to his mansion house and associates with neighbours of the same strain, who relish nothing but hunting and a bottle—with those alone he spends his time, with those alone he converses and can away with no company whose discourse goes beyond what claret and dissoluteness inspire. Such a patriot, formed in this happy way of improvement, cannot fail, as we see, to give notable decisions upon the bench at quarter sessions and eminent proofs of his skill in politics, when the strength of his purse and party have advanced him to a more conspicuous station. To such a one truly an ordinary coffee-house gleaner of the city is an errant [genuine] statesman, as much superior to, as a man conversant about Whitehall and the Court is to an ordinary shop-keeper.[9]

Nor was Locke in his low opinion of the condition of the gentry alone among his more discerning contemporaries. Edward Waterhouse complained in 1665 that "prodigality and ill conduct of life is a great worm to the flourishing gourd of an estate."[10] Edward Chamberlayne observed in 1669: "The English, especially the *Gentry* are so much given to *Prodigality* and *Slothfulness* that Estates are oftner spent and sold than in any other country."[11] Samuel Pepys lamented: "Our gentry are grown ignorant in everything of good husbandry."[12] Finally, the fulminations against the gentry by John Evelyn, who wrote his famous *Sylva* in 1662 at the request of the Royal Society to encourage gentlemanly landholders to plant, cultivate, and protect trees as one of the basic economic resources of the kingdom, cannot be omitted from any such register of opinions. He wrote angrily of "the late impolitique *Wast*, and universal *sloth* amongst us"[13] and of "our negligence, which is by nature almost *eternal*."[14] If the English countryside were to become more productive, then the gentry must display far greater industry instead of their present "*Pride, Effeminacy* and *Luxurie*."[15] Unless landed gentlemen abandoned their "*softnesse* and *vanity*," such vices "will in time not onely *effeminate* but undo the *Nation*."[16] Any of these remarks could have been made by Locke.[17]

Had Locke believed that by and large the English gentry were acting as industrious and rational human beings should, he might never have written the *Essay*, nor for that matter *Some Thoughts*

Concerning Education. Many of his ideas were a development of those of his master Bacon, especially the doctrine of the "idols." In the *Essay* he tried to convince his readers of the necessity of purifying their understandings, of regaining in a sense the pristine innocence of childhood, and once this had been accomplished through an act of will and self-reflection, they should conduct themselves as rational, autonomous beings. The blindness afflicting the understanding could only be overcome by being acutely aware of its causes; by freeing oneself from the yoke of custom, authority, and orthodoxy; and by being critical of fashion and received opinion. If this was the first step along the path of becoming enlightened, self-directed individuals, we must next begin to live intelligently by using tested methods of reasoning and inquiry in evaluating the validity of our own ideas and those of others.[18] Self-awareness of our mental predicament and systematic procedures of verification were, then, two of the principal means recommended by Locke for the attainment of the life of reason.

By implication, at least, Locke suggested a third step for the achievement of rationality.[19] This was the creation of a free and tolerant political society conducive to unfettered inquiry, critical self-examination, and enlightened action. Locke's vagueness is all the more tantalizing because of the absolutely crucial importance of what he apparently had in mind. This is one aspect of the book that makes it so fundamentally a political, indeed a revolutionary work. Religious toleration, separation of church and state, liberty of thought and expression, and freedom of association and assembly would seem to be the social environment absolutely essential for the kind of self-analysis, open exchange of ideas, and unimpeded criticism of fashion and opinion required by Locke's stipulations for rational understanding and conduct. The individual, moreover, could not adhere to the dictates of his purified, probing, rational faculty in a society dominated by a ruler who knew no checks on his governance and was responsible to no one except himself. In addition, therefore, to a society that guaranteed the basic freedoms, there must be limited constitutional government acting as a trustee of the citizens for their security and well-being, if men were to fulfill their rational potentials.

Locke wrote the *Essay*, however, not simply as an implied warning against tyranny. He was also cautioning his gentlemanly readers to act intelligently and to mend their ways or be the losers in the very practical and immediate sense of forfeiting their power and authority to those of lower station who had learned to be industrious and rational. As any confirmed Baconian recognized, knowledge was judged by its fruits, and the knowledge in this case was the wherewithal to act rationally with industry, preserverance, and enterprise, thereby enabling the individual of superior social position to dominate his inferiors. But if the inferiors could acquire more rational understanding and greater knowledge than their masters, the latter would be forced to surrender their power and privilege. The industrious and rational would inherit the earth, and ultimately birth, rank, and office must submit to superior understanding. Locke left no doubt in the minds of his audience about their fate unless they took his words to heart:

> But this, at least, is worth the consideration of those who call themselves Gentlemen, That however they may think Credit, Respect, Power, and Authority the Concomitants of their Birth and Fortune, yet they will find all these still carried away from them, by Men of lower Condition who surpass them in Knowledge. They who are blind, will always be led by those that see, or else fall into the Ditch: and he is certainly the most subjected, the most enslaved, who is so in his Understanding.[20]

From the standpoint of the thesis that Locke was a theorist of early agrarian capitalism the most relevant features of the *Essay* were its "egalitarian" doctrine and the portrait of the ideal individual that can be abstracted from its pages. The egalitarianism was compounded of several of Locke's deepest convictions. He was convinced that no authority or orthodoxy, except the principles of the law of nature and the basic tenets of Christianity, was so sacred as to be immune to challenge and criticism. All men, even the most exalted, respected, and powerful, were fallible and prone to err, and their knowledge, like that of lesser men, was flawed by a fundamental frailty. Ordinary practical men had contributed more to a civilized way of life than all the learned scholars throughout the centuries, testimony to which had been the crucial discoveries and inventions like iron, gunpowder, the compass, and quinine. Locke was a social environmentalist, discounting birth and genetic inheritance in the makeup of human beings. All men, savage and civilized, noble and humble, rich and poor, were born with approximately equal natural ability. Their later diverse talents and abilities resulted from differences in up-bringing, education, and social environment. A Hottentot trans-planted at birth to the appropriate household in England and raised as a member of the family might on maturity display all the qualities of a gentleman. The radical nature for the time of Locke's egalitar-ianism should not be underestimated.

His egalitarianism, nevertheless, might be described as "bour-geois" egalitarianism, a mentality—in opposition to the traditional aristocratic *Weltanschauung*—that came to typify the outlook of many capitalists and would-be capitalists. It was far different from the conventional aristocratic attitude that often found support in Aris-totelian doctrine with its emphasis on good birth, natural superiority and inferiority, and a gentlemanly ethic of "great souledness." Nev-ertheless, while it entailed leveling traits, Locke's egalitarianism was decidedly not meant in a democratic sense. Although he ascribed human inequality to differences in education and social environment, he accepted as desirable those differences and the social division of labor and property differentials that produced inequality. In this respect, his attitude was very much in keeping with the typical "bourgeois" egalitarianism that attacked the dominance of aris-tocratic birth, for instance, but had no intention of undermining the sovereignty of the propertied classes in general over the laboring poor. Locke, therefore, was by no stretch of the imagination a dem-ocrat, despite his belief that most men through self-help and diligent application were capable of improvement and that the most lowly person might rise above his station. Locke accepted the existing structure of society characterized by a hierarchy of class and status and a system of wide property differentials, but he also thought that the able and intelligent, regardless of birth and rank, should not be prevented from advancement. Locke's point of view certainly did not threaten the status quo, but it was obviously a significant leavening agent. The *Essay* as the *locus classicus* of this kind of outlook in the next century and a half appears to have had a signal role in shaping the consciousness of the new capitalist classes in Britain and North America.

The ideal of a human being that can be found in the *Essay* is a practical, down-to-earth, tough-minded individual, always cleaving to the useful, who will act on these egalitarian assumptions. He is a self-directed person, taking nothing on faith (except the essence of Christianity and the moral dicta of the law of nature), never conforming to fashion, custom, and received opinion, and always critical of authority and orthodoxy. Just as labor and industry are essential to the accumulation of property and its development, so they are basic to the cultivation and productivity of the rational understanding. Locke postulated a morality of mental labor, central to which was the model of the industrious, persevering, enterprising, innovative, frugal, and sober worker. Although mental labor is superior to physical work, the latter should be respected and never scorned or shunned since our very existence, well-being, and civilized way of life depend on it. Locke's position, again, is quite in keeping with the bourgeois mentality in which it is the capitalist who is "productive," rather than the laborer himself, as opposed to the idle and unproductive, "consuming" rentier aristocrat. The respect for "labour" expressed by Locke, therefore, has a very particular meaning, in addition to his desire to persuade the laborer to be industrious and accept his calling. Locke proves to have been the apostle of the strenuous life, a life perpetually beset by uneasiness and desire that from his perspective served as a necessary spur to constant endeavor, the conscientious and dedicated pursuit of one's calling, and self-betterment. Through moderation and the exercise of will, immediate and often shortsighted and detrimental desires can be suspended for the sake of a more lasting gratification in the future. Prudent and self-disciplined, Locke's hero would never indulge in mere acquisitiveness or the insatiable chase after power and riches but would pursue self-interest in a reasonable, enlightened, and Christian manner. His approach to life is shrewd, analytic, and calculating, something like balancing a ledger, totaling up credits and debits and then acting to cut his losses and enlarge his profits in the long run. Here, then, is the full characterization of the industrious and rational appropriator of chapter 5 of the *Second Treatise.*

Locke's new-model gentleman, as one discovers clues to his nature scattered through the *Essay*, substantially differs from the traditional ideal found in books that for so long had been the standard manuals for gentlemanly deportment. One has only to realize how far removed Locke's ideal is from that upheld as an example for youth in Xenophon's *Anabasis* and *Cyropaideia*, Aristotle's *Nicomachean Ethics*, and Cicero's *De officiis*. The values cherished by these ancients, whose works since at least the sixteenth century had been the staple educational diet of young English gentlemen, included a disdain for physical labor, trade and commerce, and the practically useful and an emphasis on "great souledness" or magnanimity, generosity and liberality, nobility, grace, and courage. Such qualities, by way of contrast, were virtually missing from Locke's vocabulary. Instead, he usually stressed mental and manual labor, the practical and useful, industry, perseverance, enterprise, thrift, and sobriety. The gulf separating the two outlooks was basically that between a traditional "warrior ethic" and a modern "work ethic," each involving a different notion of the meaning of rational conduct. Perhaps more than anything else Locke's ideal recalls the original "capitalist spirit" or entrepreneurial ethos so carefully identified, depicted, and analyzed in relation to the changing material conditions of early modern society by scholars like Werner Sombart, Max Weber, Ernst Troeltsch, R. H. Tawney, and Joseph Schumpeter. Locke's ideal was certainly compatible with the agrarian capitalism beginning to dominate the English countryside, and with the reflection of that important economic development in his writings.

Some Thoughts Concerning Education, actually ready for publication in the year that the *Essay* came from the press but not issued until 1693, was explicitly designed by Locke to be the practical application of his philosophic principles.[21] Profoundly worried by the "early Corruption of Youth . . . now become so general a Complaint,"[22] Locke dedicated the book to his close friend, the prosperous Somerset landowner and Whig M. P., Edward Clarke of Chipley, for the express purpose of guidance in the upbringing of his heir.[23] In general, however, the work was intended to be of aid to gentlemen in the instruction of their children on whose future the "Welfare and Prosperity of the Nation" so much depended.[24] While all youths must be educated according to their "several Conditions," Locke wrote, in order "to produce vertuous, useful, and able Men in their distinct Callings," the offspring of gentlemen should be of paramount concern: "For if those of that Rank are by their Education once set right, they will quickly bring all the rest into Order."[25]

Locke, therefore, composed one of his most widely circulated and influential works precisely to mold the attitudes and conduct of those who were in the future to be responsible for spearheading the far-reaching agricultural developments that even then were gradually transforming the English countryside from reliance on a traditional mode of production to a more advanced form of agrarian organization and enterprise. In his contribution to correcting the corruption of socially privileged youth, he was participating in an historical process that was changing the traditional self-satisfied country gentleman, often living beyond his means and devoting his ample leisure to the pursuit of pleasure, into a tough, practical-minded, frugal, and innovating agrarian capitalist. Locke could scarcely have been aware that his efforts were helping to lay the foundations not only of British world dominion but also of industrial capitalism that was to come to the fore a century and a half later. In addition to this relationship between the *Education* and the economic writings and chapter 5, therefore, another unifying link has been identified between those works and the philosophy, since one of Locke's objectives in many of the detailed recommendations for the upbringing of the young gentleman was to produce in him the very characteristics of the human ideal revealed in the *Essay*.

Among these recommendations are a number that are directly relevant to the thesis being propounded. Locke suggested that the gentlemanly youth, once he had become acquainted with natural philosophy, should be exposed to books on *"Husbandry, Planting, Gardening."*[26] French and Latin (in that order) were a requisite, as was riding.[27] Gentlemen should acquire a manual skill for recreation such as painting, woodworking, gardening, tempering, and working with iron.[28] For the young country gentleman gardening and husbandry were particularly suitable leisure-time pursuits, which would not only result in many useful things but also in the future would enable him to supervise his gardener.[29] A section of the book dealt with how the ancients fully understood that manual occupations like agriculture, husbandry, and gardening could be reconciled with an active life of affairs, and the examples cited were Gideon, Cincinnatus, Cato Major, and Cyrus the Great.[30] Locke then asserted that digging a garden, planting, and grafting by budding, or as he called them *"Delving, Planting, Inoculating,"* in addition to being useful could also constitute recreation just as much as idle games and sports.[31]

Locke's anxiety over the corruption of the landed gentry, as we have seen, was shared by some of his more far-sighted contemporaries. He was not alone in rejecting the traditional disdain of his class for manual labor and practical utility, or in calling for greater industry and less frivolous indolence among the gentry. Nor were his recommendations for the educational correction of gentlemanly corruption entirely original. Long before, John Evelyn had prescribed as indispensable to the landed gentleman the attainment of a sound knowledge of agricultural science and practical skill in husbandry that would entail actual physical work. In his *Sylva* Evelyn praised the ancients—among them Solomon, Cyrus, Numa, Lincinius, Cato, Cincinnatus—for their lack of contempt for agriculture and the cultivation of their holdings with their own hands.[32] Today, he observed, the situation was quite different. Distinguished men who themselves had not hesitated to engage in agriculture felt that the vocation was undignified for their sons, who had been raised to be gentlemen. They, in turn, ashamed of the labor and industry of their fathers, devoted themselves to pleasure, leaving the working of their estates to the most "ignorant *Hinds* and *Servants*, who are (generally speaking) more fit to Learn than to Instruct."[33] The result was that "our *Lands* are so ill *Cultivated*." Because husbandry is an art or science, Evelyn asserted that the more learning we possessed the better qualified we were to cultivate and improve our estates, adding that there was "nothing more becoming and worthy of a Gentleman" than this art. His book, Evelyn therefore claimed, was written primarily "for the encouragement of an *Industry*, and worthy *Labour*, too much in our dayes *neglected*, as haply reputed a *Consideration* of too sordid and vulgar a nature for *Noble Persons*, and Gentlemen to busie themselves withal, and who oftner find wayes to *Fell down*, and Destroy their *Trees* and *Plantations*, than either to *repair* or improve them."[34] His words must have had the desired effect, for he said in the dedication to the king of the second edition that, on the basis of the responses he had received to the first edition, he estimated that over two million timber trees and many other kinds had been planted.[35] Obviously, he had succeeded "not to persuade *Men* to sit still, and let Nature work alone, but to ayd and assist *her*."[36]

If Locke, in a somewhat less direct and forceful fashion than Evelyn, conveyed the same message, he went beyond his predecessor on one point. Regardless of the stigma customarily attached to trade and commerce by gentlemen, they should adopt the merchants' system of double-entry accounting to keep track of their own expenses and so help to prevent themselves from living extravagantly beyond

their means, a procedure that one day might also save them from
bankruptcy:

> *Merchant's Accompts*, though a Science not likely to help a Gentleman to
> get an Estate, yet possibly there is not any thing of more use and efficacy,
> to make him preserve the Estate he has. 'Tis seldom observed, that he who
> keeps an Accompt of his Income and Expences, and thereby has constantly
> under view the course of his domestick Affairs, lets them run to ruine: And
> I doubt not but many a Man gets behind-hand, before he is aware, or runs
> further on, when he is once in, for want of this Care, or the Skill to do it.
> I would therefore advise all Gentlemen to learn perfectly *Merchant's Ac-
> compts*, and not to think it is a Skill, that belongs not to them, because it has
> received its Name, and has been chiefly practised by Men of Traffick.[37]

The passage, whose significance cannot be exaggerated, patently
expressed the rational, calculating approach to ordinary life so much
an essential part of the capitalist spirit. Of even greater importance
is the fact that Locke prescribed the method of the countinghouse for
the landed gentleman in the management of his estate. Therefore, in
writing his treatise on education Locke evidently hoped to prepare
gentle youth for the calling of landholder by imbuing them with
something of the spirit of capitalism. Once again we are back full
circle to the industrious and rational cultivators of their divine inheritance.

If these were some of Locke's attempts to reform the gentry,
making them into sturdy pillars of the economy and a fit ruling class,
his stipulations for the education of the poor were quite different in
substance and tone.[38] Locke wrote his "project about the better relief
and employment of the poor" in 1697 while serving as a commissioner of the Board of Trade.[39] He seems to have taken the subject
of the memorandum very seriously, judging from the comment to
Edward Clarke: "It is a matter that requires every Englishman's best
thoughts; for there is not any one thing that I know upon the right
regulation whereof the prosperity of his country more depends. And
whilst I have any breath left I shall always be an Englishman."[40] His
aim was to mobilize the unemployed, force them by unrelenting
draconian methods to labor, and shape them into a docile and defer-
ential brigade instilled with the work ethic of industry, thrift, and
sobriety. They would thus be better able to serve their reformed
masters by more efficiently improving the landed estates of England,
thereby increasing profits and rents. Little of Christian charity or
compassion for the less fortunate can be found in this unusually

harsh document, so severe, in fact, that its recommendations were never adopted by the Board of Trade.

Locke began the paper with the assertion that the growth of the unemployed was not so much due to the lack of subsistence or job opportunities as it was to the "relaxation of discipline and corruption of manners." Since "vice and idleness" had so overcome "virtue and industry" among many of the "herd," an initial step must be taken in "restraint of their debauchery" by strict enforcement of the law in closing "superfluous brandy shops and unnecessary ale houses." The question of "begging drones" and "idle vagabonds" was most urgent. To remedy the appalling conditions in which "the streets everywhere swarm with beggars, to the increase of idleness, poverty, villainy, and to the shame of Christianity," Locke proposed a new law as well as the severe application of the existing ones. All males between the ages of fourteen and fifty caught begging outside their own parish without a pass in maritime counties should be impressed for three years of service in His Majesty's ships, and those so apprehended who were married or over fifty should be committed to three years of hard labor in the nearest house of correction. Boys and girls under the age of fourteen begging outside their parish without a pass should be "soundly whipped," and on second offence girls over fourteen should serve three months of hard labor in a house of correction. Anyone counterfeiting a pass ought on first offence to have his ears cut off and on second offence should be transported to the colonies. Each able-bodied unemployed laborer should be compelled to work by the local guardians of the poor, who would arrange a job for him at wages lower than customarily paid because his condition implied a "defect in his ability or honesty." Refusal to accept such forced employment in a maritime county should be penalized by impressment for three years, and elsewhere by confinement in a house of correction.

The "true and proper" relief of the poor, those able and willing to labor, "consists in finding work for them, and taking care they do not live like drones upon the labour of others." Locke gave special attention to two groups of these poor: infirm people and wives of day laborers still able to do something for their own support, for instance by part-time work with wool, and children under fourteen who constituted an excessive burden on parish poor relief. Both categories, especially the children, could be cared for, Locke proposed, by a nationwide system of "working schools" to be instituted and administered by the parishes. The working schools would be for all children between the ages of three and fourteen of families on parish relief, who eventually at no cost to the parish would be able by spinning or knitting or performing other functions in wool manufacture to cover the cost of their daily bread and, in cold weather, to defray the expense of warm-water gruel: "The same fire that warms the room may be made use of to boil a pot of it." At the age of fourteen apprentices would be recruited from their number for nine-year terms for work on the land or other occupations, the additional two years beyond the normal seven-year contract introduced as an enticement to local employers for taking advantage of the arrangement. Adults, presumably the infirm and wives of laborers freed of caring for their children during the day, would also be eligible to work in the schools. The schoolchildren would be "kept in much better order, be better provided for" than at home, and as adults they would become "sober and industrious," having grown accustomed to work from their earliest years. Moreover, they would have been indoctrinated with the Christian virtues because of compulsory church attendance with their school masters and mistresses.

Some of Locke's later writings, therefore, can be interpreted in part as constituting elements of a "project," rooted in his earlier social and political analysis, whose purpose was to resuscitate and promote the interests of the English state and nation. Leadership and economic initiative would be provided by a landed gentry, reformed and invigorated by the proper upbringing and education, that would oversee and direct a mass of laborers, rendered dutiful and industrious by revised poor laws. The conduct of these recreated landed proprietors and direct economic producers would by and large be "rational." Locke, however, never intended to equate the rationality of the enterprising country gentleman with the rationality of the diligent, conscientious manual worker. Both would be rational, but rationality varied by rank and station. The day laborer, sincerely dedicated to his calling, Bible-reading and God-fearing, and committed to self-improvement was, from Locke's point of view, certainly rational according to his rights. His rationality, however, differed from that of the individual who had benefited from education, leisure, the opportunity to travel and discuss his ideas, who did not constantly have to struggle in back-breaking toil for survival, and who used his advantage to improve himself and contribute positively to the welfare of state and country. A few from the lower orders might, of course, through their own ability and character rise in the social scale, and they were to be encouraged, commended, and rewarded. Nevertheless, Locke's vision of a rational society, at least from what can be understood of it, remained one of basic inequalities, of rank and privilege, and of wide property differentials, dominated by a small minority of enlightened landed gentry.

CHAPTER SEVEN

Conclusion

Even a strictly limited social history of Locke's political theory, such as the one just attempted, by situating some of his ideas in their appropriate contexts has been able to call attention to a few previously unnoticed aspects of his thought. This kind of "payoff" would alone justify employing the historical mode of analysis more than it has been used in the past. The central question animating the inquiry is how Locke's social and political ideas were related, if at all, to a number of basic characteristics of his society. Late seventeenth-century England was still predominantly an agricultural nation in which landed property was essential to wealth, power, and social position. Economic behavior continued to be motivated to a great extent not by profit but by such noneconomic factors as custom, tradition, and prestige. Mercantile and manufacturing capitalism were fairly restricted in scope, and full-time wage labor in these sectors was an exception. The beginnings of a self-regulating market society had appeared, but no truly national market would exist for another century. Basic organizational and technological changes were transforming agrarian structure with the result that in the specialized corn and mixed corn and livestock areas of the south and east family subsistence agriculture was being replaced by capital farms. The rise to prominence of agrarian capitalism in these parts of the countryside was accompanied by crucial changes in the social relations of production such as the concentration of land holdings in ever larger estates in the hands of ever fewer proprietors, the increasing separation of direct producers from control of the means of production, the growing commodification of labor, and the emergence of the rural triad of landed rentier, capitalist tenant farmer, and wage laborer. The capitalist farmers, at this time quite possibly of greater total wealth than their commercial and manufacturing counterparts and certainly exceeding them in number, typically displayed a rational business attitude to their calling, maximizing profits by reinvestment in order to increase productivity. Since mid-century an increasing number of agricultural treatises and manuals were being published, many of them written by Baconian-inspired reformers who stressed technical innovation and improvement and the vital importance of individual labor and industry, and who dealt generally with the means of increasing productivity, the problems of waste land, and the advantages of enclosure. More and more socially concerned Englishmen were becoming alarmed by the corruption of traditionally minded landed gentlemen—their imprudent living beyond their means in luxury and indolence—and warned of the danger to the common interest unless they mended their ways. Finally, some enterprising individuals were applying the Baconian method of natural history to the study of social problems, foremost among them being the exponents of "political arithmetic," who were creating the new sciences of political economy and demography.

How, then, did these interrelated historical phenomena help shape Locke's social and political ideas? How was his thought an expression or reflection of them? Can the meaning of many of the propositions of Locke's various texts be comprehended without reference to them? These are queries to which little or no attention has been given, yet they are problems to which the answers must be found if Locke as a social and political thinker is to be understood. They are especially relevant questions since Locke wrote for the instruction of his contemporaries in their practical affairs, employed the language of the agricultural reformers, and dealt with some of the most pressing social issues of his age. If the facts and the questions about their possible relationship to Locke's social and political thought are ignored by those who cleave to a philosophical analysis of a text more or less divorced from the historical circumstances, then a considerable burden of proof is definitely on them to demonstrate exactly and in some detail why such features of English society are of little or no relevance to the understanding of his ideas.

One further illustration should be given of the way in which the study of political thought may be somewhat altered by adopting the approach of social history. Hobbes has usually been a favorite of those scholars who treat the classic texts from the standpoint of the philosophical mode of analysis. Judged to be the greatest English philosophical work, Hobbes's *Leviathan* is often given more attention than Locke's *Second Treatise*. This is because the thinker of Malmesbury dazzles the reader by the brilliance of his logically rigorous and systematic thought and his trenchant, incisive prose. Locke is sometimes represented not as having constructed an intellectual *tour de force* like *Leviathan*, which raises a host of tantalizing philosophical problems, but as a rather slipshod, pedestrian political thinker who is simply no match, either substantively or stylistically, for the agile and beguiling mind of Hobbes. Locke, of course, might have been Hobbes's inferior in scoring points in a senior commonroom debate. Yet from the standpoint of the social history of political thought it is Locke who is probably the more significant figure. For it is through Locke rather than Hobbes that a fuller picture can be obtained of what was happening in English society, and it was Locke rather than Hobbes who seemed more aware of those developments that were to have such basic consequences in the shaping of our own society. While no one could reasonably belittle Hobbes's stature as a political theorist or fail to relish his philosophical achievement, he tended to be a backward-looking thinker whose ideas, fascinating as they are, lead off the main road to the future. Hobbes, moreover, given some of the specific problems with which he was wrestling and his conception of absolute sovereign power, seemed less at home in the English than in the French tradition of political thought extending back through Bodin to the beginning of the fourteenth century.[1] Locke, on the other hand, recently described by an intellectual historian as "perhaps the most English of English philosophers,"[2] dealt more directly and realistically with the English experience. Locke, not Hobbes, was the hard-headed realist more in tune with the social and political actualities of the time and place. In view of the fact that Britain in a century and a half was to raise the standard for the rest of the world to follow by becoming the first industrial capitalist state, a development to which Locke contributed in a not insignificant way, he rather than Hobbes might possibly be labeled the first modern political thinker. Locke turned his back on the past in a number of important ways and took the road to the future.

My intention in this study has been to indicate something of this character of Locke's political thought by identifying two categories of his social and political ideas: those elements that in themselves do not suggest an incipient theory of agrarian capitalism but are supportive of it, and those notions that are essential to such a theory. In the first group, precedence perhaps should be given to Locke's view that all members of political society should have the rights of life, liberty, and possessions underwritten by the law of nature. The chief purpose of government is the protection and security of these rights. Nevertheless, the right to landed property (and other rights), although guaranteed by the law of nature, is not an unconditional and absolute right. Government can legitimately regulate landed property for the public good, that is, the equal preservation of the lives, liberties, and possessions of all. No one, however, can be deprived of his property in violation of the law of nature and without the consent of the community. Locke also expounds a labor theory of property, and he approves of the use of money as giving tacit consent to wide property differentials and in expanding exchange relationships. Stress is placed on the critical function of agriculture in the economy and on the importance of the landed gentry and necessity of their living within their incomes by observing thrift, industry, and sobriety. Merchants, speculators, and middlemen are criticized for being unproductive drones, for removing money from circulation. When taken together these selected themes would certainly entitle Locke to be called a theorist of an agricultural society. While it is extremely dangerous to argue that the meaning of a political thinker can be found in the common interpretation given to his work by contemporaries and near-contemporaries, those who most closely shared his values and language, it was precisely in this way that he was conceived of by eighteenth-century English "commonwealthmen" and the Scottish natural jurists.[3] For them Locke was the classic theorist of landed society and the landholder, not of commerce and mercantile interests.

However true this may be, and at least it is partial confirmation of my thesis, there is more of significance in Locke. He was indisputably a theorist of landed men and property but also of a society beginning to be transformed by agrarian capitalism, bringing with it changes expressed in his thought. Unless this is admitted, how do we explain the source of those novel features of his attitude toward agriculture and the social relations of production in the countryside, ingredients pointing to future developments on a vast scale? Keeping this in mind, we would immediately have to point to his triadic conception of agrarian organization: landlord, tenant, and worker, whose respective incomes were rents, profits, and wages. Related to the idea of triadic structure is his notion of the rural wage-laborer, so different from slave, serf, and traditional free artisan. Locke seems to have been unperturbed by the increasing separation of the agricultural worker from ownership or control of farm land in England, and he began to envisage labor in general as a commodity to be exchanged for wages in the market. He takes for granted that the worker, a juridically free man, who is forced to live at a mere subsistence level, will for the sake of survival seek in his own neighborhood or abroad to sell his labor to the highest bidder. The emphasis given to productivity and improvement is also crucial, as is the related justification for enclosure and exploitation of waste land. His opinion that the value of a commodity to an important degree depends on the labor it embodies is applied to land. The foundation of the English economy is not land alone but its value from the standpoint of productivity. If land values are high, everything else being equal, the economy is strong and vigorous. High rents mean high land values. Ultimately high rents are determined by the labor and productivity of the tenant farmers and their ability consequently to increase profits by the extraction of surplus value from the workers.

This second category of ideas shows that Locke was considerably more than a theorist of an agricultural society. He was, in fact, a theorist of a special type of agricultural society emerging in England. In his writings he abstracted a new kind of agricultural society from its coexistence with a traditional agrarian sector and presented it as a theory of the whole. The perception of the beginning of a transformation in the social relations of agricultural production then occurring in England, when coupled with a human ideal of a practical-minded, self-interested, autonomous, and calculating individual, specifically entitle Locke to be described as a theorist of a developing agrarian capitalism and, in a broader sense, a pioneer of the spirit of capitalism.

Notes

CHAPTER ONE

1 This chapter is designed mainly for historians of political thought who are political scientists by training. To the professional historian much of it may appear to belabor the obvious. For my views on methodology, also see "The Social History of Political Theory," *Political Theory*, 6 (August 1978), pp. 345–67; and Ellen Meiksins Wood and Neal Wood, *Class Ideology and Ancient Political Theory: Socrates, Plato, and Aristotle in Social Context* (New York: Oxford University Press, 1978), chap. 1.

2 For one example of how "history from below" may aid a better understanding of a classic political theorist, see my essay "African Peasant Terrorism and Augustine's Political Thought," to be published in the forthcoming *Festschrift* in honor of George Rudé, edited by Frederick Krantz.

3 As examples of such scholarship one need only think of the skillful and insightful work of John Plamenatz, Judith Shklar, Charles Taylor, and Sheldon Wolin.

4 For example, Perry Anderson, Peter Brown, Alfred Cobban, M. I. Finley, Peter Gay, Christopher Hill, G. E. M. de Ste. Croix, Keith Thomas, and Brian Tierney are such historians whose work bears on questions of political theory.

5 C. B. Macpherson, *The Political Theory of Possessive Individualism: Hobbes to Locke* (Oxford: Clarendon Press, 1962); Quentin Skinner, *The Foundations of Modern Political Thought*, 2 vols. (Cambridge: Cambridge University Press, 1978).

115

6 For an example in contrast to Macpherson, see Keith Thomas, "The Social Origins of Hobbes's Political Thought," in *Hobbes Studies*, ed. K. C. Brown (Oxford: Blackwell, 1965), pp. 185–236; and my article, "Thomas Hobbes and the Crisis of the English Aristocracy," *History of Political Thought*, 1 (Autumn 1980), pp. 437–52.

7 The most important of these for our purposes are: Quentin Skinner, "Meaning and Understanding in the History of Ideas," *History and Theory*, 8 (1969), pp. 3–53; "'Social Meaning' and the Explanation of Social Action," in *Philosophy, Politics and Society*, 4th ser., ed. Peter Laslett, W. G. Runciman, and Quentin Skinner (Oxford: Blackwell, 1972), pp. 136–57; "Some Problems in the Analysis of Political Thought and Action," *Political Theory*, 2 (August 1974), pp. 277–303.

   Useful guides to the methodology are: Cary J. Nederman, "Historical Method in the Study of Political Thought: Beyond Quentin Skinner's Unhistorical 'History'"; James H. Tully, "The Pen Is a Mighty Sword: Quentin Skinner's Approach to the Study of Political Theory." Both are unpublished papers given respectively in 1981 and 1982 at the annual meeting of the Canadian Political Science Association.

8 Although Skinner does not use the term *paradigm*, his debt to Thomas S. Kuhn's analysis of the history of science seems obvious.

9 Skinner, *Foundations*, vol. 1, pp. 349–52.

10 *Episodic* is the apt term used by Nederman in his valuable analysis, "Historical Method." In addition to the treatment of Machiavelli in *Foundations*, Skinner subsequently published *Machiavelli* (London: Oxford University Press, 1981). On Hobbes see Skinner, "The Context of Hobbes' Theory of Political Obligation," in *Hobbes and Rousseau*, ed. M. Cranston and R. S. Peters (Garden City, N.Y.: Doubleday-Anchor, 1972), pp. 109–42; "Conquest and Consent: Thomas Hobbes and the Engagement Controversy," in *The Interregnum: The Quest for Settlement, 1646–1660*, ed. G. E. Aylmer (London: Archon Books, 1972), pp. 79–98.

11 For an incisive criticism of the revisionists, see T. K. Rabb, "The Role of the Commons," *Past and Present*, 92 (August 1981), especially pp. 75–76.

12 James Tully, *A Discourse on Property: John Locke and His Adversaries* (Cambridge: Cambridge University Press, 1980); see chaps. 4–5 of this book.

CHAPTER TWO

1 C. B. Macpherson, *The Political Theory of Possessive Individualism: Hobbes to Locke* (Oxford: Clarendon Press, 1962), chap. 5; Leo Strauss, *Natural Right and History* (Chicago: University of Chicago Press, 1950), pp. 202–51. Macpherson's basic interpretation of Locke was worked out in two articles published much earlier than his book: "Locke on Capitalist Appropriation," *Western Political Quarterly*, 4 (December 1951), pp. 550–66; "The Social Bearing of Locke's Political Theory," *Western Political Quarterly*, 7 (March 1954), pp. 1–22. Also on Locke see the essay in his *Democratic Theory: Essays in Retrieval* (Oxford: Clarendon Press, 1973), chap. 13, reprinted from *Political Theory and the Rights of Man*, ed. D. D. Raphael (London: Macmillan, 1967).

2 Peter Laslett, "Introduction," in Locke, *Two Treatises of Government* (Cambridge: Cambridge University Press, 1960), pp. 42–44. On pp. 103–6, specific issue is taken with Macpherson's 1951 position and with Leo Strauss. Laslett's views seem not to have substantially altered in his second edition of the *Two Treatises* (1970). In addition, see his "John Locke, the Great Recoinage, and the Origins of the Board of Trade, 1695–1698," in *John Locke: Problems and Perspectives: A Collection of New Essays*, ed. John W. Yolton (Cambridge: Cambridge University Press, 1969), pp. 157–58.

3 John Dunn, *The Political Thought of John Locke: An Historical Account of the Argument of the "Two Treatises of Government"* (Cambridge: Cambridge University Press, 1969), p. 255. Also see the criticisms in Alan Ryan, "Locke and the Dictatorship of the Bourgeoisie," *Political Studies*, 13 (1965), pp. 219–30; and Martin Seliger, *The Liberal Politics of John Locke* (London: Allen and Unwin, 1968), especially pp. 141–44.

4 Keith Tribe, *Land, Labour and Economic Discourse* (London: Routledge and Kegan Paul, 1978), p. 51.

5 James Tully, *A Discourse on Property: John Locke and His Adversaries* (Cambridge: Cambridge University Press, 1980), p. 138.

6 Although it is not within the scope of this essay to examine in detail the historical reasons for the early agricultural developments and the rise of agrarian capitalism in England, something by way of introduction must be said on the subject. On the origins of English agrarian capitalism I have done little more than condense portions of Robert Brenner's superb analysis, "The Agrarian Roots of European Capitalism," *Past and Present*, 97 (November 1982), es-

pecially pp. 76–113. Other relevant articles by Brenner are: "Agrarian Class Structure and Economic Development in Pre-Industrial Europe," *Past and Present*, 70 (February 1976), pp. 30–75; "The Origins of Capitalist Development: A Critique of Neo-Smithian Marxism," *New Left Review*, 104 (July-August 1977), pp. 25–42.

In addition to Brenner, the following have proved useful on English agriculture in general and on capitalist agriculture in particular during the sixteenth and seventeenth centuries: Joyce Oldham Appleby, *Economic Thought and Ideology in Seventeenth-Century England* (Princeton: Princeton University Press, 1978); Mildred Campbell, *The English Yeoman Under Elizabeth and the Early Stuarts* (New Haven: Yale University Press, 1942); G. E. Fussell, *The Classical Tradition in West European Farming* (Rutherford, N.J.: Fairleigh Dickinson University Press, 1972); Fussell, *The Old English Farming Books from Fitzherbert to Tull, 1523 to 1730* (London: Crosby Lockwood, 1947); H. J. Habakkuk, "English Land-ownership, 1680–1740," *Economic History Review*, 10 (1940), pp. 2–17; Eric Kerridge, *The Agricultural Revolution* (London: Allen and Unwin, 1967); Kerridge, *The Farmers of Old England* (London: Allen and Unwin, 1973); Ann Kussmaul, *Servants in Husbandry in Early Modern England* (Cambridge: Cambridge University Press, 1981); Rowland Edmund Prothero, Baron Ernle, *English Farming, Past and Present*, introductions by G. E. Fussell and O. R. McGregor, 6th ed. (London: Heinemann and Frank Cass, 1961); Sir E. John Russell, *A History of Agricultural Science in Great Britain, 1620–1954* (London: Allen and Unwin, 1966); Lawrence Stone, *The Crisis of the Aristocracy, 1558–1641* (Oxford: Clarendon Press, 1965); Stone, *Family and Fortune: Studies in Aristocratic Finance in the Sixteenth and Seventeenth Century* (Oxford: Clarendon Press, 1973); Joan Thirsk, ed., *The Agrarian History of England*, vol.4, *1500–1640* (Cambridge: Cambridge University Press, 1967); Thirsk, *Economic Policy and Projects: The Development of a Consumer Society in Early Modern England* (Oxford: Clarendon Press, 1978); Thirsk, "Seventeenth-Century Agriculture and Social Change," in *Land, Church, and People: Essays Presented to Professor H. P. R. Finberg*, ed. Joan Thirsk, *Agricultural History Review*, 18, suppl. (1970), pp. 148–77; Charles Webster, *The Great Instauration: Science, Medicine and Reform, 1626–1660* (London: Duckworth, 1975).

7 *Republica*, I, chap. 23, p. 74.

8 A relevant *Oxford English Dictionary* definition of *farmer*: "One who rents land for the purpose of cultivation; = *tenant farmer*."

9 G. E. Fussell, ed., *Robert Loder's Farm Accounts, 1610–1620*, Camden Society, 3rd ser., vol. 53 (London: Royal Historical Society, 1936), pp. xxiii–vi, quoted in Gordon Batho, "Noblemen, Gentlemen and Yeomen," in Thirsk, ed., *Agrarian History*, p. 303.

10 Kerridge, *Farmers of Old England*, chap. 3.

11 Locke's political thought, therefore, must be clearly distinguished from Hobbes's. See my "Thomas Hobbes and the Crisis of the English Aristocracy," *History of Political Thought*, 1 (Autumn 1980), especially p. 452.

12 E. P. Thompson, "The Peculiarities of the English," in his book *The Poverty of Theory and Other Essays* (London: Merlin, 1978), especially pp. 40–45. This essay was originally published in *The Socialist Register 1965*, ed. Ralph Miliband and John Saville, pp. 311–62. Actually, Thompson refers to English agrarian capitalists as a "bourgeoisie" only on pp. 40 and 43, and by using "capitalist" generally he avoids the confusion that I am cautioning against below.

13 Maurice Cranston, *John Locke: A Biography* (New York: Macmillan, 1957), p. 6.

14 Kerridge, *Agricultural Revolution*, pp. 121–22, 253, 261; *Farmers of Old England*, p. 90; Campbell, *English Yeoman*, p. 172.

15 Cranston, *Locke*, p. 17.

16 Kerridge, *Agricultural Revolution*, p. 121. In a region of capital farms like Somerset where the expensive technique of water meadows was used to increase productivity, the position also must have been of importance. John Evelyn, *Terra*, p. 40, contended that such watering has "been found one of the richest improvements that ever was put in practice."

17 Cranston, *Locke*, p. 115.

18 Ibid., p. 70. Locke's letters to his three successive "managers," his uncle Peter Locke, cousin William Stratton, and Cornelius Lyde, in *Correspondence* are ample evidence for this conclusion.

19 K. H. D. Haley, *The First Earl of Shaftesbury* (Oxford: Clarendon Press, 1968), p. 220.

20 L. F. Brown, *The First Earl of Shaftesbury* (New York: Appleton-Century, 1933), p. 136.

21 Thirsk, ed., *Agrarian History*, p. 65.

22 Eric Kerridge, "Agriculture, c. 1500–1793," in *V. C. H. Wiltshire*, vol. 4 (London, 1959), pp. 57 ff., quoted in Brenner, "Agrarian Roots," p. 95.

23 Thirsk, ed., *Agrarian History*, pp. 493, 537, 559.

24 W. D. Christie, *A Life of Anthony Ashley Cooper, First Earl of Shaftesbury*, vol. 2 (London: Macmillan, 1871), pp. 49–51, 418; Brown, *First Earl of Shaftesbury*, pp. 230–31; Haley, *First Earl of Shaftesbury*, p. 250.

25 Christie, *Life of Shaftesbury*, vol. 2, pp. 61, 220–21.

26 *Works*, vol. 9, pp. 323–56.

27 *Correspondence*, no. 528.

28 Brown, *First Earl of Shaftesbury*, pp. 163 ff.; Haley, *First Earl of Shaftesbury*, pp. 249–50; David Hawke, *The Colonial Experience* (Indianapolis: Bobbs-Merrill, 1976), especially pp. 212–13.

29 Laslett, "Introduction," *Two Treatises of Government*, p. 29 n. Laslett's emphasis is on colonial administration. On Locke, Worsley, and Slingsby he refers to P. Kelly, *The Economic Writings of John Locke*, diss. University of Cambridge, 1969.

30 On Worsley, see G. E. Aylmer, *The State's Servants: The Civil Service of the English Republic, 1649–1660* (London: Routledge and Kegan Paul, 1973), pp. 270–72; Brown, *First Earl of Shaftesbury*, pp. 141–44; Haley, *First Earl of Shaftesbury*, pp. 255–59; and the numerous references in Webster, *Great Instauration*.

31 For Worsley's views on agriculture, see Christie, *Life of Shaftesbury*, vol. 2, appendix 1, which is a paper, probably written in 1668, in the past attributed to Shaftesbury but now thought to be written by Worsley. See Laslett, "John Locke, the Great Recoinage," p. 143 and n. 3. The source of the paper is *Shaftesbury Papers*, XLIX, 8. Christie's transcription should be read with the corrections noted in Haley, *First Earl of Shaftesbury*, p. 257 n. 3. Also see Webster, *Great Instauration*, appendix 5, for a short anonymous work, "Proffits Humbly Presented to This Kingdome," which Webster believes to have been written by Worsley in 1647.

32 On Slingsby, see William Letwin, *The Origins of Scientific Eco-*

nomics: English Economic Thought, 1660–1776 (London: Methuen, 1963), pp. 104, 163.

33 See the transcription of the manuscript in H. R. Fox Bourne, *The Life of John Locke*, vol. 1 (London: King, 1876), pp. 222–27.

34 On these reformers, see Webster, *Great Instauration*, chaps. 1, 5–6. For Locke's intellectual debt to Bacon and Baconianism, see my article, "The Baconian Character of Locke's *Essay*," *Studies in History and Philosophy of Science*, 6 (1975), pp. 43–84; and my book, *The Politics of Locke's Philosophy: A Social Study of "An Essay Concerning Human Understanding"* (Berkeley and Los Angeles: University of California Press, 1983), especially chaps. 2, 5–6.

35 Webster, *Great Instauration*, p. 469.

36 See Francis Bacon, *Sylva sylvarum* (London, 1627), pars. 401–676.

37 Bacon, *Sylva sylvarum*, pars. 401–12. Russell, *History of Agricultural Science*, pp. 16–18. John Evelyn, *Terra*, pp. 38–39, refers to Bacon as an authority on soil. Evelyn (1620–1706), a fellow of the Royal Society, was always a staunch Anglican and Royalist, and he should not be numbered among Hartlib's circle of improvers. He wrote on various agricultural subjects and translated several works on gardening from the French. Locke knew him, but he evidently did not own a copy of his classic, *Sylva*.

38 Webster, *Great Instauration*, p. 483.

39 Weston was a Catholic and Royalist who had made his peace with the Government.

40 Samuel Hartlib, *Samuel Hartlib His Legacy of Husbandry*, 3rd ed. (London, 1655), pp. 110–11, quoted in Webster, *Great Instauration*, p. 474.

41 Webster, *Great Instauration*, pp. 57–67; Charles Webster, "The Authorship and Significance of Macaria," in *The Intellectual Revolution of the Seventeenth Century*, ed. Charles Webster (London: Routledge and Kegan Paul, 1974), p. 379.

42 Webster, *Great Instauration*, p. 59.

43 Quoted in Russell, *History of Agricultural Science*, p. 20.

44 Webster, "Macaria," p. 375 and n. 19.

45 Ibid., p. 385.

46 Quoted in Russell, *History of Agricultural Science*, p. 26.

47 Locke's other association with Wilkins was as a member of his Latitudinarian circle in London in the mid-sixties. See Barbara J. Schapiro, *John Wilkins, 1614–1672: An Intellectual Biography* (Berkeley and Los Angeles: University of California Press, 1969), pp. 154–55.

48 On Wilkins's agricultural interests, see ibid., p. 197; and Webster, *Great Instauration*, pp. 162–63.

49 For the Georgical Committee, see Reginald Lennard, "English Agriculture Under Charles II: The Evidence of the Royal Society's 'Enquiries,'" *Economic History Review*, 4 (October 1932), pp. 23–45; Michael Hunter, *Science and Society in Restoration England* (Cambridge: Cambridge University Press, 1981), pp. 92–93.

50 For what follows on Locke's library, I have relied on John Harrison and Peter Laslett, *The Library of John Locke*, 2nd ed. (Oxford: Clarendon Press, 1971). On the books themselves, Campbell, Fussell, Prothero, Russell, and Webster are valuable guides.

51 On Grew, Mayow, and Woodward, see Russell, *History of Agricultural Science*, pp. 34–36. Locke evidently was a friend of Woodward. See Woodward to Locke, 6 January 1696, *Correspondence*, no. 1994. Evelyn, *Terra*, p. 4, refers to the "ingenious Dr. Woodward."

52 Webster, *Great Instauration*, p. 473.

53 For the complex publishing history of Weston's book, see Fussell, *Old English Farming Books*, pp. 41–44. Webster, *Great Instauration*, p. 520, cites Arthur Young's belief that Weston's contribution to civilization was more important than Newton's.

54 A recent appraisal of Dymock's scheme for farm layout is that of J. A. Yelling, *Common Field and Enclosure in England, 1450–1850* (London: Macmillan, 1977), pp. 121–23.

55 Harrison and Laslett, *Library of Locke*, pp. 26–27. Also see Kenneth Dewhurst, *John Locke (1632–1704) Physician and Philosopher: A Medical Biography with an Edition of the Medical Notes in His Journals* (London: Wellcome Historical Medical Library, 1963), pp. 8–9. Dewhurst claims that Locke "collected about 1,600 specimens."

56 See John Lough, ed., *Locke's Travels in France, 1675–1679: As Re-*

lated in His Journals, Correspondence and Other Papers (Cambridge: Cambridge University Press, 1953).

57 Ibid., pp. xxvii–viii.

58 Ibid., pp. 88–89, 147–48, 207–8, 236–37.

59 Ibid., p. 89.

60 For example, *Correspondence*, nos. 449, 524, 658, 1775, 1785.

61 *Correspondence*, nos. 465, 559, 573, 626, 658, 663, 670, 774, 788, 813, 822, 872, 951, 1080, 1083, 1086, 1371, 1894.

62 *Correspondence*, nos. 580, 586, 589, 597, 623, 776, 808, 813, 822, 872, 875, 924, 1086, 1371, 1844, 1845, 1847, 1853, 2813.

63 *Correspondence*, no. 776.

64 *Correspondence*, nos. 981, 989.

65 *Correspondence*, nos. 1371, 1769. Also see Cranston, *Locke*, p. 343; Harrison and Laslett, *Library of Locke*, p. 9.

66 *Correspondence*, nos. 1844, 1845, 2813.

67 *Correspondence*, nos. 876, 924, 1080, 1083, 1086, 1768, 1844, 1847, 2447.

68 *Correspondence*, no. 844. Cf. *Education*, $ 193.

69 *Correspondence*, no. 999. Cf. *Education*, $ 204.

70 *Correspondence*, no. 878.

CHAPTER THREE

1 *Some of the Consequences That Are Like to Follow upon Lessening of Interest to 4 Percent*, which hereafter will be referred to as a work of 1668 and cited *1668*, although the last few pages in William Letwin's transcription, 297–300 (manuscript pp. 28, 28b, 29, 29b, 30, 30b, 31, 31b), were signed and dated in 1674, and Locke himself thought of it as a writing of that year. See the quotation that follows this note in the text. All citations of these 1674 additions

will be so indicated in subsequent footnotes. The published expansion of 1692, cited as *1692, Some Considerations of the Consequences of the Lowering of Interest and Raising the Value of Money. In a Letter Sent to a Member of Parliament, 1691*, appeared in December 1691. Its date of publication by Awnsham and John Churchill was 1692, however, and will so be considered. See Maurice Cranston, *John Locke: A Biography* (New York: Macmillan, 1957), p. 350 and n. 1. Locke, *1692*, p. 3, indicated that the writing had been completed a year before he dated the preface, November 7, 1691, which meant that it was probably composed in the autumn of 1690, the year of the publication of the *Essay* and the *Two Treatises*, and of the completion of *Some Thoughts Concerning Education*.

2 *1692*, p. 4. The reference seems to be to 1674.

3 For example, James Tully, *A Discourse on Property: John Locke and His Adversaries* (Cambridge: Cambridge University Press, 1980).

4 Richard Ashcraft, "Revolutionary Politics and Locke's *Two Treatises of Government:* Radicalism and Lockean Political Theory," *Political Theory*, 8 (November 1980), pp. 429–86. See chap. 4 of the present work.

5 Locke's broad economic outlook is often mistakenly called mercantilistic. See the perceptive study by K. I. Vaughan, *John Locke: Economist and Social Scientist* (Chicago: University of Chicago Press, 1980), especially chap. 3.

6 *Essay Concerning Toleration*, pp. 187, 194. Cf. *Toleration*, pp. 125–27.

7 *1668*, p. 278.

8 *1668*, p. 278.

9 *Journal, BL. MS Locke*, c. 30, fols. 18 and 19, quoted in Richard H. Cox, *Locke on War and Peace* (Oxford: Clarendon Press, 1960), pp. 175–76.

10 *Second Treatise*, §§3, 95, 107, 131; *Toleration*, pp. 125–27.

11 *1692*, p. 13.

12 Vaughan, *Locke*, p. 121, concludes that "it would be an exaggeration to claim that Locke was . . . an advocate of a policy of laissez-faire."

13 For the background to the 1668 manuscript and 1692 treatise and some of the technical economic issues involved, see: Joyce Oldham Appleby, *Economic Thought and Ideology in Seventeenth-Century England* (Princeton: Princeton University Press, 1978), pp. 221–41; Cranston, *Locke*, pp. 350 ff.; William Letwin, *The Origins of Scientific Economics: English Economic Thought, 1660–1776* (London: Methuen, 1963), chap. 6; Eric Roll, *A History of Economic Thought*, 4th ed. (London: Faber and Faber, 1973), pp. 112–16; Joseph A. Schumpeter, *History of Economic Analysis*, ed. Elizabeth Boody Schumpeter (New York: Oxford University Press, 1954), pp. 298–99, 316–17, 328–32; Vaughan, *Locke*, chaps. 2–3.

14 Petty's volume was first published in 1662. There seem to be no fundamental textual differences between the two issues. The 1667 edition has been used throughout since it was the one Locke most likely read. Locke was to acquire a good collection of Petty's later works. On Petty, see E. A. J. Johnson, *Predecessors of Adam Smith* (New York: Prentice Hall, 1937), chap. 6; Letwin, *Origins of Scientific Economics*, chap. 5; Guy Routh, *The Origin of Economic Ideas* (London: Macmillan, 1975), pp. 35–46; Emil Strauss, *Sir William Petty: Portrait of a Genius* (London: Bodley Head, 1954); and the many references in Charles Webster, *The Great Instauration: Science, Medicine and Reform, 1626–1660* (London: Duckworth, 1975).

15 Schumpeter, *History of Economic Analysis*, p. 213.

16 On Baconian natural history the following should be consulted: Michael Hunter, *Science and Society in Restoration England* (Cambridge: Cambridge University Press, 1981), chap. 1; Charles Webster, *Great Instauration*, especially pp. 420–27, 447–49; John W. Yolton, *Locke and the Compass of Human Understanding* (Cambridge: Cambridge University Press, 1970), pp. 4–5, 58–59, 62–63, 74–77, 86–89, 103.

17 Webster, *Great Instauration*, p. 423.

18 Ibid., p. 421.

19 On political arithmetic, in addition to the sources cited in n. 14, see Peter Buck, "Seventeenth-Century Political Arithmetic: Civil Strife and Vital Statistics," *Isis*, 68 (1977), pp. 67–84; Hunter, *Science and Society*, pp. 121–22, 210–11; Shichiro Matsukawa, "Origin and Significance of Political Arithmetic," *Annals of the Hitotsubashi Academy*, 6 (1955), pp. 53–79.

20 Locke had two editions of Graunt's classic, and Potter's *Humble proposals* . . . (London, 1651). He possessed a 1674 edition of Collin's *An Introduction to Merchants' Accounts* and two of his later works: *Plea for the Bringing in of Irish Catle* (London, 1680), and *Salt and Fishery* (London, 1682).

21 Volumes by Wood in Locke's library were: *Times Mended* (London, 1681) and *A New Almanac* (London, 1680). For Wood's earlier views on decimalization and monetary theory see Webster, *Great Instauration*, pp. 416–20, 449–54, and appendix 4.

22 Peter Laslett, "John Locke, the Great Recoinage, and the Origins of the Board of Trade," in *John Locke: Problems and Perspectives: A Collection of New Essays*, ed. John W. Yolton (Cambridge: Cambridge University Press, 1969), p. 144, n. 1. When Locke first met Petty, who died in 1687, is unknown.

23 Locke to William Molyneux, 23 November 1694, *Correspondence*, no. 1817.

24 See chap. 2 in the present volume.

25 The phrase *"Number, Weight, or Measure"* is used by Petty in *Political Arithmetick* (London, 1690), preface, to denote his quantitative method. It is found with a similar quantitative meaning in Bacon, *Novum organum* (1620), XCVIII, and in Gerard Malynes, *Consuetudo, Vel Lex Mercatoria, or The Ancient Law-Merchant* (London, 1622), "Epistle to the Reader." However, the phrase, apparently taken from the Wisdom of Solomon, originally signified the divine order and harmony of the universe and was employed in this sense during the Middle Ages. On this point, see Buck, "Political Arithmetic," pp. 74, 75; Letwin, *Origin of Scientific Economics*, p. 130; Matsukawa, "Political Arithmetic," p. 73.

26 Quoted in Matsukawa, "Political Arithmetic," p. 75.

27 *1668*, pp. 275, 278, 282, 297 (added in 1674).

28 *Political Arithmetick*, preface.

29 Quoted in Matsukawa, "Political Arithmetic," p. 58.

30 Quoted in Ibid., pp. 58–59.

31 Charles Davenant, *Discourses on the Publick Revenues* (1698), part 1, p. 13, quoted in Letwin, *Origin of Scientific Economics*, p. 113.

32 *Treatise*, pp. 17–18.

33 *Treatise*, pp. 25, 47, 56, 67.

34 *Treatise*, pp. 16, 25, 47, 59.

35 *Treatise*, chap. 4.

36 *Treatise*, pp. 18, 20–21, 31–34, 35, 64.

37 *Treatise*, pp. 35, 64, 71.

38 *Treatise*, p. 10.

39 *Treatise*, pp. 23–24, 29, 30, 31, 66–67.

40 *Treatise*, pp. 4, 16.

41 *Treatise*, pp. 12, 32, 36, 39.

42 *1668*, p. 278.

43 *1668*, p. 287.

44 For some expression of this awareness, see *1692*, p. 19. John
Houghton wrote in 1681: "And seeing that what the Husbandman
is concern'd for, is the *Materia prima* of all Trade; and that the
finding a vent for his Commodities, is as necessary to his end, as it
is to know the ways of Tilling, Planting, Sowing, Manuring, ordering, and improving of all sorts of Gardens, Orchards, Meadows,
Pastures, Corn-Lands, Woods, and Coppices; as also of Fruits,
Corn, Grain, Pulse, new Hays, Cattel, Fowl, Beasts, Bees, Silkworms, etc. . . . . therefore I design not only to give Instructions for
that end, but also the best accounts I can meet with, how they
may be advantageously parted with; which will necessitate me often to treat of such things as more strictly come under the second
Head of my Title, *viz.* Trade," *Letters*, vol. 1, pp. 2–3.
    The little known Houghton (1640–1705) was a London apothe-
cary and tea merchant who became a fellow of the Royal Society in
1680. His *Letters* was the first agricultural periodical, to be followed by a weekly in 1692–1703. Contributors to the earlier journal included Evelyn, Charles Howard, brother of the duke of Norfolk, and John Worlidge, author of *Systema agriculturae* (1669).
Bernard A. Keen, *The Physical Properties of the Soil* (London:
Longmans, Green, 1931), pp. 8–9, calls an experiment conducted
by Houghton the "first recorded account of any attempt to classify

soils on the basis of particle size," and hence "the tentative beginning of a new epoch in the study of soil."

45 *1668*, p. 283.

46 *1692*, p. 28.

47 *1692*, p. 62.

48 *1668*, p. 297 (added in 1674); and *1692*, p. 46. Also see *1668*, pp. 284–85, 286–87, 291, 292, 293, 295; *1692*, pp. 31–32, 34–36, 40–41, 43, 47, 93. This was the standard unit of value given by the classical political economists. Appleby, *Economic Thought*, p. 57, says that, after 1662, "increasingly, grain appears in economic tracts as a commodity interchangeable with other commodities."

49 *1668*, p. 283.

50 *1692*, pp. 73–74.

51 *1692*, p. 71.

52 *1692*, pp. 54–61.

53 Cf. *1668*, p. 283, with *1692*, pp. 28–29.

54 Schumpeter, *History of Economic Analysis*, pp. 322–23; also Vaughan, *Locke*, pp. 54 ff.

55 *1692*, p. 60; also pp. 20, 72.

56 *1692*, p. 67.

57 *1668*, pp. 280–81; *1692*, pp. 54–55, 56, 61, 72, 75, 76, 97. Also see Locke, *Further Considerations Concerning Raising the Value of Money* (1695), in *Works*, vol. 4, p. 166.

58 *1692*, p. 56.

59 Adam Smith, *An Inquiry into the Nature and Causes of the Wealth of Nations*, ed. R. H. Campbell and A. S. Skinner; textual editor, W. B. Todd (Oxford: Clarendon Press, 1976), I, vi, 11, 17, 20; xi, 7, 8; II, ii, 1.

60 *1668*, pp. 278, 288; *1692*, pp. 36–37.

61 *1668*, p. 296.

62 *1668*, pp. 275–76, 278, 280, 282–83, 287, 288, 300 (added in 1674); *1692*, pp. 16, 21–29, 49, 50, 57, 58, 70–71, 73.

63 *1668*, pp. 276, 300 (added in 1674); *1692*, pp. 16, 24, 25, 28, 29, 50, 57, 73.

64 *1668*, p. 280; *1692*, pp. 24–25, 58. References in Locke's other works to "day labourer" are: *First Treatise*, ∮44; *Second Treatise*, ∮41; *Essay*, IV, xx, 3; *Conduct*, pp. 39, 50; *Reasonableness*, pp. 146, 157. Although "day labourer" is not used in *Poor Laws*, this is what Locke is thinking of on p. 381. It perhaps is suggestive that in *Conduct*, p. 39, Locke juxtaposes "day labourer in a country village," "low mechanic of a country town," and "porters and cobblers of great cities"; and in *Reasonableness*, p. 146, he writes of "day-labourers and tradesmen." The seventeenth-century meaning of *tradesman* was "artisan" or "craftsman" as well as "shopkeeper" or "merchant." "Day labourer" in the *Two Treatises* as cited above would seem to signify agricultural worker.

65 *1692*, pp. 28–29. The only works in which Locke refers more frequently to "servant" appear to be: *First Treatise*, ∮∮130, 135; *Second Treatise*, ∮∮2, 24, 28, 29, 77, 85, 86; *Education*, ∮∮18, 19, 39, 59, 68, 70, 76, 83, 89, 117. The references in *Education*, as one might expect, are clearly all to domestics; those in the *Two Treatises* are either in a broad sense to all laborers or seemingly to domestics or servants in husbandry, although these latter two meanings are usually difficult to distinguish.

66 *1692*, pp. 28–29.

67 See Georges Duby, *The Three Orders: Feudal Society Imagined*, trans. Arthur Goldhamn.er, foreword by T. N. Bisson (Chicago: University of Chicago Press, 1980), especially pp. 42–43, 105, 158–60, 274.

68 *Oxford English Dictionary*. This is the first definition given. Examples are from Milton, Phillips, Addison, and Arthur Young.

69 *Republica*, I, chap. 16, p. 65; chap. 23, p. 74; III, chap. 8, p. 141.

70 *Republica*, I, chap. 24, p. 76.

71 *Treatise*, pp. 31–32, 64.

72 *Treatise*, pp. 35, 71.

73 *1668*, p. 280; *1692*, pp. 24–25. Also see *Second Treatise*, ∮85: "A

Free-man makes himself a Servant to another, by selling him for a certain time, the Service he undertakes to do, in exchange for Wages he is to receive." See chap. 5 of the present volume.

74 On this point and particularly on task work see E. P. Thompson's illuminating essay, "Time, Work-Discipline, and Industrial Capitalism," *Past and Present*, 38 (December 1967), pp. 56–97.

75 M. E. Seebohm, *The Evolution of the English Farm* (Cambridge, Mass.: Harvard University Press, 1927), p. 267.

76 On the question of servants in husbandry, see the recent excellent study on which I have extensively relied, Ann Kussmaul, *Servants in Husbandry in Early Modern England* (Cambridge: Cambridge University Press, 1981).

77 *1692*, p. 25.

78 *1668*, p. 300 (added in 1674); *1692*, p. 50; *Further Considerations*, in *Works*, vol. 4, p. 148. In the latter passage, he specifies those "in any labour."

79 *Republica*, I, chap. 24, p. 76. An indispensable treatment of the subject is Christopher Hill, *Change and Continuity in Seventeenth-Century England* (London: Weidenfeld and Nicolson, 1974), chap. 10, "Pottage for Freeborn Englishmen: Attitudes to Wage-Labour." The essay originally appeared in *Socialism, Capitalism, and Economic Growth: Essays Presented to Maurice Dobb*, ed. C. H. Feinstein (Cambridge: Cambridge University Press, 1967).

80 Edward Chamberlayne, *Angliae Notitia, or the Present State of England*, 3rd. ed. (London, 1669), pp. 444–45; quoted in Kussmaul, *Servants in Husbandry*, p. 8.

81 *1668*, p. 280; *1692*, pp. 24, 57, 71. Also, Petty, *Treatise*, pp. 35, 64. Elsewhere Locke refers to the "poor" and "poor and wretched" day laborer, and to his "ordinary drudgery." See *Reasonableness*, p. 157; *Essay*, IV, xx, 3; *Conduct*, p. 50. From what Locke says in *Conduct*, p. 39, the day laborer is intellectually inferior to other kinds of manual workers: "The day labourer in a country village has commonly but a small pittance of knowledge because his ideas and notions have been confined to the narrow bounds of a poor conversation and employment; the low mechanic of a country town does somewhat outdo him; porters and cobblers of great cities surpass them." On Locke's general attitude toward workers, also see E. J. Hundert, "The Making of

Homo Faber: John Locke Between Ideology and History," *Journal of the History of Ideas*, 33 (1972), especially pp. 6–7; "Market Society and Meaning in Locke's Political Philosophy," *Journal of the History of Philosophy*, 15 (January 1977), especially pp. 33–34, 36–37, 39–43.

82 *Political Arithmetick*, preface.

83 *1692*, p. 36.

84 *1692*, p. 73.

85 *1692*, p. 71.

86 See chap. 6 in the present volume.

87 For what follows in the text, see Joan Thirsk, "Seventeenth-Century Agriculture and Social Change," in *Land, Church, and People: Essays Presented to Professor H. P. R. Finberg*, ed. Joan Thirsk, *Agricultural History Review*, 18, suppl. (1970), pp. 148–177.

88 *1692*, p. 19.

89 *1692*, pp. 33–34, 65. On Romney Marsh, or "Rumney-marsh" as Locke usually called it, the vast marshlands near Rye, see Eric Kerridge, *The Agricultural Revolution* (London: Allen and Unwin, 1967), pp. 134–36; *The Farmers of Old England* (London: Allen and Unwin, 1973), pp. 54, 79, 91, 96, 118. Also see the comment by Child on "Rumsey marsh" in *Large Letter*, pp. 40–41.

90 *1692*, p. 4

91 *1668*, p. 278.

92 *1668*, p. 288.

93 *1692*, pp. 15, 20, 37, 39, 53, 54, 55, 59, 61, 71, 72, 73, 74, 75.

94 *1692*, pp. 19–20.

95 *1692*, p. 20.

96 *1692*, p. 72.

97 *Robert Loder's Farm Accounts, 1610–1620*, Camden Society, 3rd ser., vol. 53 (London: Royal Historical Society, 1936); and *Rural*

Economy in Yorkshire in 1641, Being the Farming and Account Books of Henry Best, ed. C. B. Robinson, Surtees Society, vol. 33 (Durham: G. Andrews, 1857).

98 *1692*, especially pp. 24–25, 54–55, 66, 69–73, 79.

99 Kerridge, *Agricultural Revolution*, pp. 345–48.

100 *1692*, pp. 54–55, 66, 79. Elizabeth is mentioned in all three passages; James I on pp. 66, 79; and Charles I on p. 66.

101 Kerridge, *Agricultural Revolution*, p. 346. Also see H. J. Habakkuk, "La Disparation due paysan anglais," *Annales*, 20 (1965), pp. 657–58, and p. 657, n. 3.

102 *1692*, p. 53.

103 *1692*, pp. 55, 57, 61, 72, 75, 76, 97.

104 Hunter, *Science and Society*, p. 110.

105 Ibid., p. 122. The work by Nehemiah Grew, British Library MS Lansdowne 691, was probably written in 1707 and is titled: *The Meanes of a Most Ample Encrease of the Wealth and Strength of England in a Few Years Humbly Represented to her Majestie in the Fifth Year of Her Reign*. Although I have not seen the manuscript, there is an excellent summary in Johnson, *Predecessors of Smith*, chap. 7. According to Johnson (p. 119), Grew was a friend of Petty.

106 Johnson, *Predecessors of Smith*, p. 134.

107 Quoted in ibid.

108 See chap. 6 in the present volume.

CHAPTER FOUR

1 E. J. Hundert, "The Making of Homo Faber: John Locke Between Ideology and History," *Journal of the History of Ideas*, 33 (1972), p. 11; K. I. Vaughan, *John Locke: Economist and Social Scientist* (Chicago: University of Chicago Press, 1980), p. 131; also, pp. 110–11.

2 Locke to Richard King, 25 August 1703, *Works*, vol. 9, p. 308. Laslett begins the introduction, p. 3, to his edition of the *Two Treatises* with this quotation.

3 James Tully, *A Discourse on Property: John Locke and His Adversaries* (Cambridge: Cambridge University Press, 1980). It should be pointed out that Tully, p. 149, thinks that *Some Considerations* "is a letter of advice" and not a work of economic analysis. Whatever the meaning of this cryptic remark, he does not attempt to relate the work to the *Second Treatise*.

4 See Richard Ashcraft's important article, "Locke's State of Nature: Historical Fact or Moral Fiction?," *American Political Science Review*, 62 (September 1968), pp. 898–915.

5 *Essay*, II, i. 2. Bacon, *Great Instauration*, "Plan of the Work," in Bacon, *Works*, ed. J. Spedding, R. L. Ellis, and D. D. Heath, vol. 4 (London: Longmans, 1887–1901), pp. 26–27.

6 *Second Treatise*, ⸹49.

7 See Ronald L. Meek, *Social Science and the Ignoble Savage* (Cambridge: Cambridge University Press, 1976), especially chap. 1.

8 *Second Treatise*, ⸹⸹26, 28, 30, 37, 45, 46.

9 *Second Treatise*, ⸹38.

10 *Second Treatise*, ⸹⸹32, 33, 34, 45.

11 *Second Treatise*, ⸹⸹35, 38, 48.

12 Ronald Meek sees Grotius and Pufendorf as other basic sources of the four-stage theory. Locke was especially important because of his view that contemporary American Indians were the pattern of development of the first Europeans and Asians (*Second Treatise*, ⸹⸹49, 108), and because of his conception in the *Essay* of the mind as *tabula rasa*. Meek quite rightly thinks that Locke and Pufendorf, on the basis of the biblical account of Cain and Abel (*Second Treatise*, ⸹38), believed the first three stages to have coexisted from the very beginning. Unlike Pufendorf, however, Locke, due to his stress on the American Indians (and it might be added, due to the emphasis given to Abraham's pastoral mode of subsistence in *Second Treatise*, ⸹38), offered something approaching a developmental sequence of the first three stages. It is also clear that for Locke the primitive agricultural stage was followed by a more advanced stage

involving production for exchange and profit, that is, commerce. This latter stage, at least in chapter 5, seems to be characterized by the exchange of agricultural rather than manufactured commodities.

13 *Second Treatise,* §§28, 30, 32–51.

14 *Second Treatise,* §§28, 30, 35, 36, 37, 41, 42, 43, 45.

15 *Second Treatise,* §§41, 42, 43.

16 *Second Treatise,* §43.

17 *Second Treatise,* §§25, 26, 27, 31, 32, 34, 35, 38, 39.

18 Robert Filmer, *Patriarcha and Other Political Works,* ed. Peter Laslett (Oxford: Blackwell, 1949), p. 187. The quotation is from the preface to *Observations upon Aristotles Politiques Touching Forms of Government . . .* (1652).

19 Gordon J. Schochet, *Patriarchalism in Political Thought: The Authoritarian Family and Political Speculation and Attitudes Especially in Seventeenth-Century England* (New York: Basic Books, 1975), pp. 137–38.

20 See in particular Samuel Pufendorf, *De jure naturae et gentium libri octo* (1672), II, ii; IV, iv–v. The pagination used below is that of Samuel Pufendorf, *Of the Law of Nature and Nations,* trans. into English with Jean Barbeyrac's notes, 2nd ed. (Oxford, 1710).

21 Ibid., pp. 81–87.

22 Ibid., pp. 289–93.

23 *First Treatise,* §53; *Second Treatise,* §§6, 56.

24 *Second Treatise,* §§27–28, 45.

25 *Law of Nature,* p. 201.

26 *Law of Nature,* pp. 207, 215.

27 *Law of Nature,* p. 213; *Essay,* IV, iii, 18; *Education,* §110.

28 *Law of Nature,* pp. 157, 173; *First Treatise,* §§86, 88.

29 *Second Treatise,* §§134, 135, 139; also *Law of Nature,* p. 157; *Education,* §116.

30 *Toleration*, pp. 65, 67, 89, 91.

31 *Essay Concerning Toleration*, p. 183; *Toleration*, pp. 67, 125, 127, 129.

32 *Second Treatise*, §§139, 140, 142.

33 *Second Treatise*, §§165, 200; *Toleration*, p. 103.

34 *Second Treatise*, §135.

35 *Toleration*, pp. 103 ff., 131 ff.; *Essay Concerning Toleration*, p. 178.

36 *Second Treatise*, §27. In regard to the natural law limitations, I am mainly following Macpherson's insightful analysis, which I believe to be fundamentally correct, and I use his terminology. See C. B. Macpherson, *The Political Theory of Possessive Individualism: Hobbes to Locke* (Oxford: Clarendon Press, 1962), pp. 199–220.

37 *Second Treatise*, §§23, 24, 85, 196.

38 *First Treatise*, §130.

39 *Second Treatise*, §85; also §§28–29. Any discussion of this thorny question will be deferred until chap. 5 in the present volume.

40 *First Treatise*, §§43, 130; *Second Treatise*, §§24, 69, 85–86. Vaughan, *Locke*, p. 156, n. 17, comments: "Given Locke's doctrine, I can see nothing absurd or incredible in his putting wage labor in the state of nature."

41 *Second Treatise*, §27.

42 *Second Treatise*, §§31, 33, 36, 37.

43 *Second Treatise*, §31.

44 *Second Treatise*, §§36, 37, 45–50.

45 *Second Treatise*, §34.

46 *Second Treatise*, §48.

47 *Second Treatise*, §37.

48 *Second Treatise*, §§40–42.

49 *Second Treatise*, §§45, 50.

50 *Second Treatise,* ⸗28, 29, 36, 50, 77, 85.

51 *Second Treatise,* ⸗49.

52 *Second Treatise,* ⸗50.

53 *Second Treatise,* ⸗131.

54 *First Treatise,* ⸗⸗33, 41.

55 *Second Treatise,* ⸗32.

56 *Second Treatise,* ⸗34.

57 Joyce Oldham Appleby, *Economic Thought and Ideology in Seventeeth-Century England* (Prnceton: Princeton University Press, 1978), p. 69.

58 Blith, *English Improver,* p. 4; Austen, *Spirituall Use,* "Epistle Dedicatory"; Reeve, *Directions,* "Epistle Dedicatory"; Boyle, *Usefulnesse,* pp. 24–25.

59 Blith, *English Improver,* pp. 5–6; also Reeve, *Directions,* "Epistle Dedicatory."

60 *Terra,* p. 2.

61 *Usefulnesse,* p. 43.

62 *Usefulnesse,* p. 19.

63 *Usefulnesse,* p. 20.

64 *Second Treatise,* ⸗⸗32, 35, 36.

65 G. E. Fussell, *The Old English Farming Books from Fitzherbert to Tull, 1523 to 1730* (London: Crosby Lockwood, 1947), pp. 74–75, 79–80.

66 *Second Treatise,* ⸗32.

67 *Second Treatise,* ⸗37.

68 *Second Treatise,* ⸗42.

69 *Second Treatise,* ⸗⸗32, 40.

70 *Second Treatise*, ₰₰40, 44. Other sections in which Locke used *improve* or a variant are: ₰₰33, 34, 41.

71 *Second Treatise*, ₰₰34, 36, 37, 42, 43, 45, 46, 48.

72 *Treatise*, p. 47.

73 For example, Blith, *English Improver*, "Epistle Dedicatory to Parliament," "Epistle to the Ingenuous Reader"; also p. 9; Blith, *English Improver Improved*, "Epistle Dedicatory to Cromwell"; Dymock, *New Divisions*, pp. 8–9; Weston, *Discours*, "To My Sons." Also see Evelyn, *Sylva*, "To the Reader," pp. 120, 131–32.

74 *English Improver*, "Epistle to the Ingenuous Reader."

75 *Kalendarium*, p. 5. Also on his attitude to labor, see chap. 6 of the present volume.

76 Mildred Campbell, *The English Yeoman Under Elizabeth and the Early Stuarts* (New Haven: Yale University Press, 1942), pp. 376 ff. Of particular relevance is Richard Baxter's last work, *The Poor Husbandman's Advocate* (1691). Baxter was interested in science and was a great admirer of Bacon and Boyle. See N. H. Keeble, *Richard Baxter: Puritan Man of Letters* (Oxford: Clarendon Press, 1982), pp. 43, 48, 108–9.

77 *Second Treatise*, ₰34.

78 *Second Treatise*, ₰36.

79 *Second Treatise*, ₰37.

80 Campbell, *English Yeoman*, pp. 171–72.

81 Ibid., p. 172.

82 *Second Treatise*, ₰42.

83 *Second Treatise*, ₰42.

84 *Second Treatise*, ₰43.

85 *Second Treatise*, ₰48.

86 Joan Thirsk, "Seventeenth-Century Agriculture and Social Change," in *Land, Church, and People: Essays Presented to Professor*

H. P. R. Finberg, ed. Joan Thirsk, *Agricultural History Review*, 18, suppl. (1970), pp. 156–57.

87 *Second Treatise*, §§35, 38, 40, 42, 45.

88 *Second Treatise*, §42.

89 *Treatise*, pp. 4, 16; *Political Arithmetick*, chaps. 1, 4; Appleby, *Economic Thought*, pp. 133, 136, 137, 154.

90 Thirsk, "Seventeenth-Century Agriculture," p. 169.

91 Quoted in Joan Thirsk, *Economic Policy and Profits: The Development of a Consumer Society in Early Modern England* (Oxford: Clarendon Press, 1978), p. 180.

92 *Letters*, vol. 1, pp. 10–11.

93 Quoted in E. A. J. Johnson, *Predecessors of Adam Smith* (New York: Prentice-Hall, 1937), p. 133.

94 Ibid., p. 136.

95 In the *Second Treatise, appropriation*: §§26, 28, 29, 32, 33, 35, 36, 37; *enclosure*: §§26, 32, 33, 35, 37, 38, 48; *common land*: §§27–30, 32, 34, 35, 38, 39, 40, 44, 45, 46, 48, 51; *waste land*: §§36, 37, 38, 42, 43, 45, 49.

96 On this last point, see *Second Treatise*, §35.

97 *Second Treatise*, §49.

98 *Second Treatise*, §§28, 35.

99 *Sylva*, p. 208.

100 *Second Treatise*, §36.

101 *Second Treatise*, §42.

102 *Second Treatise*, §37.

103 *Second Treatise*, §28. For a discussion of the turfs passage, see chap. 5 in the present volume.

104 *Second Treatise*, §30.

105 For seventeenth-century usage see the *Oxford English Dictonary.*

106 In general, for the conflation of common and waste land, see Rowland Edmund Prothero, Baron Ernle, *English Farming, Past and Present*, introductions by G. E. Fussell and O. R. McGregor, 6th ed. (London: Heinemann and Frank Cass, 1961), p. 124; Thirsk, "Seventeenth-Century Agriculture," pp. 167 ff.

107 *English Improver*, p. 18.

108 *Large Letter*, p. 41.

109 *New Divisions*, p. 3.

110 *Sylva*, pp. 92, 147.

111 *Large Letter*, p. 40.

112 *Letters*, vol. 1, pp. 10–11. Houghton does not accept Gerard Malynes's much earlier estimate in *Consuetudo, Vel Lex Mercatoria; or, The Ancient Law-Merchant* (London, 1622) of twelve million acres of waste out of a total of twenty-nine million.

113 Prothero, *English Farming*, p. 145.

114 Johnson, *Predecessors of Smith*, p. 121.

115 Thirsk, "Seventeenth-Century Agriculture," p. 167.

116 *Directions*, "Epistle Dedicatory."

117 For example, Reeve, *Directions*, "Epistle Dedicatory"; Weston, *Discours*, "To My Sons," p. 5 and passim; Austen, *Fruit Trees*, "Epistle Dedicatory," pp. 1–2; Child, *Large Letter*, p. 57.

118. Austen, *Fruit Trees*, "Epistle Dedicatory."

119 See the convenient summary of early enclosure in Michael Turner, *English Parliamentary Enclosure: Its Historical Geography and Economic History* (Folkestone, Eng.: Dawson-Archon Books, 1980), pp. 137–45. Also J. A. Yelling, *Common Field and Enclosure in England, 1450–1850* (London: Macmillan, 1977), chap. 1.

120 Turner, *Parliamentary Enclosure*, p. 144; Campbell, *English Yeoman*, chap. 3.

121 These few lines on fen drainage are derived from Lawrence Stone, *The Crisis of the Aristocracy, 1558–1641* (Oxford: Clarendon Press, 1965), pp. 355–57.

122 Gillingham Forest, Wiltshire-Dorset border; Braydon Forest, Wiltshire; Dean Forest, Gloucestershire; Feckenham Forest, Worcestershire; Leicester Forest. For these details on the disafforestation and the popular protests against it, see Buchanan Sharp, *In Contempt of All Authority: Rural Artisans and Riot in the West of England, 1586–1660* (Berkeley and Los Angeles: University of California Press, 1980), especially chaps. 4–5, 7–8.

123 Ibid. On the popular uprisings in the fens, see Brian Manning, *The English People and the English Revolution, 1640–1649* (London: Heinemann, 1976), pp. 126–38; also the useful discussion on enclosure of forests and wastes in Christopher Hill, *The World Turned Upside Down: Radical Ideas During the English Revolution* (London: Temple Smith, 1972), pp. 40–45.

124 In general on the arguments for enclosure see, Appleby, *Economic Thought*, pp. 59 ff; Prothero, *English Farming*, especially pp. 96–130. Specific arguments of the improvers can be found in Blith, *English Improver*, pp. 62–72, 87–89; Austen, *Fruit Trees*, "Epistle Dedicatory"; Evelyn, *Sylva*, p. 208; Dymock, *New Divisions*, pp. 3–9; Child, *Large Letter*, pp. 37, 41–42.

125 *Letters*, vol. I, pp. 15–16.

126 In this chapter no attempt has been made to present a comprehensive summary of the many arguments for enclosure. Many of them had to do with technical agricultural advantages. Evelyn's argument in his *Fumifugium; or, The Inconveniencie of the Aer and Smoak of London Dissipated* (London, 1661), pp. 23–26, seems to have been unique. In order to counteract the foul air of London, he recommended drainage and enclosure of the marshland adjacent to the metropolis, to be planted with beans, peas, and blossom-bearing grains and surrounded with gardens of fragrant plants and flowers. This was the only book by Evelyn in Locke's library. For Evelyn's views on drainage, see *Terra*, pp. 40 ff.

127 On "masterless men" in seventeenth-century England, see Hill, *World Turned Upside Down*, chap. 3. For one of the earliest recorded examples of a prolonged concern over masterless men, see my "African Peasant Terrorism and Augustine's Political Thought," to be published in the forthcoming *Festschrift* in honor of George Rudé, edited by Frederick Krantz.

128 For example, Blith, *English Improver*, pp. 65–66, 69–72; Child, *Large Letter*, p. 42; Austen, *Fruit Trees*, "Epistle Dedicatory."

129 *English Improver Improved*, "Epistle to Reader."

130 *New Divisions*, pp. 3–4, 8–9.

131 *Large Letter*, pp. 44–45.

132 *Second Treatise*, §90; also §91.

133 *Second Treatise*, §45.

134 See James Moore, "Locke and the Scottish Jurists," pp. 4–6, 17–18, a paper presented to a conference on John Locke and the political thought of the 1680s sponsored by the Conference for the Study of Political Thought, Folger Shakespeare Library, Washington, D.C., March 21–23, 1980. Jean Barbeyrac, editor and translator of Pufendorf's *De jure naturae et gentium*, published in Amsterdam in 1706, also held this view.

135 *Second Treatise*, §37.

136 *Second Treatise*, §40.

137 *Second Treatise*, §42.

138 *Second Treatise*, §43.

139 Petty, *Treatise*, pp. 25, 47, 56, 59, 67; *Political Arithmetick*, pp. 70, 96–97. Appleby, *Economic Thought*, p. 86, refers to "the refrain of turning mercury into gold through the modern alchemy of agricultural improvements."

140 Campbell, *English Yeoman*, p. 86. Evidence shows that entry fines for leases on enclosed manorial land were rated at over four times the fines on unenclosed land of the same manor.

141 Quoted in Fussell, *Farming Books*, p. 46.

142 Weston, *Discours*, "To My Sons."

143 *Discours*, pp. 20–25. Petty, *Political Arithmetick*, p. 4, refers to the scheme, calling Weston the "Author of a most Judicious discourse of Husbandry."

144 Sir E. John Russell, *A History of Agricultural Science in Great Britain, 1620–1954* (London: Allen and Unwin, 1966), p. 37.

145 *Letters*, vol. I, p. 14.

146 *Letters*, vol. I, p. 17.

147 Johnson, *Predecessors of Smith*, p. 121.

148 Ibid., p. 122.

149 For similar titles of books by improvers see Fussell, *Farming Books*, pp. 53–54.

150 *English Improver*, "Epistle Dedicatory to Parliament."

151 *English Improver*, pp. 16–17.

152 *English Improver*, p. 63.

153 Blith, *English Improver Improved*, pp. 224–26.

154 *English Improver Improved*, pp. 174–77.

155 *Large Letter*, p. 42.

156 Joseph Lee, *Considerations Concerning Common Fields and Inclosures* (1654), p. 39, quoted in Appleby, *Economic Thought*, p. 60.

157 Quoted in Prothero, *English Farming*, p. 64.

158 *Second Treatise*, ⸹41.

159 Quoted in Thirsk, *Economic Policy and Projects*, p. 118.

160 Richard Ashcraft, "Revolutionary Politics and Locke's *Two Treatises of Government*: Radicalism and Lockean Political Theory," *Political Theory*, 8 (November 1980), pp. 429–86.

161 Ibid., p. 436.

162 Ibid., p. 431.

163 Ibid., p. 456. For the common radical vocabulary, see pp. 442–45, 450–51, 469–75. It can be summarized as consisting of the following ideas: natural equality and freedom in a state of nature under natural law; natural rights of self-preservation and property, and of resistance to tyrannical rule; a distinction between the state of nature and the state of war; the foundation of civil society as a basic agreement of the people; consent of the people as fundamental to governmental authority; the end of the state as the common good. The radical vocabulary also included what Richard Ashcraft calls a "code language" devised by the

ideologues (like Locke and Robert Ferguson) to unify their cause and activate the movement, pp. 469–75: "invasion of rights," "usurpation," "tyranny," the king's "betrayal of his trust," the king's use of "force and violence," "noxious beasts," and so on.

164 Ibid., pp. 455–56.

165 "Persons of quality," that is, "gentlemen"; see for example the title of the anonymous Whig pamphlet, often attributed to Locke, *A Letter from a Person of Quality to His Friend in the Country* (1675), in *Works*, vol. 9, pp. 200–246. "Good and sober men" was a label applied by Whigs to themselves, ibid., p. 208.

166 *Ashcraft*, "Revolutionary Politics," p. 455.

167 *Letters*, vol. I, p. 15. Houghton supported the Tories during the Exclusion Crisis. See Michael Hunter, *Science and Society in Restoration England* (Cambridge: Cambridge University Press, 1981), p. 127.

168 See n. 165 in this chapter.

169 Ashcraft, "Revolutionary Politics," p. 434, states that "a prolegomena of the position to be developed in the *Two Treatises of Government* can be found in" the *Letter*. On the question of Locke's authorship of this and other Whig tracts, see Maurice Cranston, *John Locke: A Biography* (New York: Macmillan, 1957), pp. 158–59; H. R. Fox Bourne, *The Life of John Locke*, vol. 1 (London: King, 1876), pp. 336, 482, 487–88. Locke denied that he had ever authored such works. See Locke to Pembroke, 28 November/8 December 1684, *Correspondence*, no. 797; and Cranston's comments, *Locke*, pp. 247 ff.

170 *A Letter from a Person of Quality*, in *Works*, vol. 9, p. 246.

171 Ibid.

172 *Second Treatise*, §42. "Increase of lands" refers to productivity, and "right imploying" suggests policies designed to encourage and facilitate enclosure and improvement.

173 *Treatise*, p. 4.

CHAPTER FIVE

1 James Tully, *A Discourse on Property: John Locke and His Adversaries* (Cambridge: Cambridge University Press, 1980), pp. ix–x.

2 Ibid., p. 154.

3 Ibid., p. 174.

4 This is not to deny that another kind of egalitarianism can be found in Locke's thought. See chap. 6 of the present volume.

5 See chap. 3 of the present volume.

6 *Essay*, I, iv, 15; *Conduct*, pp. 81, 115; *Reasonableness*, p. 139. For a perceptive discussion of this vocabulary shared by gentlemanly authors, see Christopher Hill, *Change and Continuity in Seventeenth-Century England* (London: Weidenfeld and Nicolson, 1974), chap. 8, "The Many-Headed Monster," originally published in *From the Renaissance to the Counter-Reformation: Essays in Honor of Garrett Mattingly*, ed. C. H. Carter (New York: Random House, 1965).

7 *First Tract*, p. 158; *Reasonableness*, pp. 135, 149; *Conduct*, p. 81.

8 *Conduct*, p. 81.

9 *Conduct*, p. 82.

10 *Conduct*, p. 81.

11 *First Tract*, p. 158.

12 *Poor Laws*, p. 378. Locke is writing of the unemployed poor. See chap. 6 of the present volume.

13 *Poor Laws*, pp. 379, 381.

14 *First Tract*, p. 158.

15 *First Tract*, p. 158.

16 *Toleration*, p. 147.

17 *Conduct*, p. 81.

18 *Conduct*, p. 116.

19 *Reasonableness*, p. 146.

20 Locke to Richard King, 25 August 1703, *Works*, vol. 9, p. 308. Locke uses the expression "superficial knowledge," but it appears from the context that "superficial" is not meant in the pejorative

sense of shallow, trivial, or careless. Rather, Locke seemed to think that Smith's book lacked the detail for a "full insight" into the constitution. Moreover, Smith was dated as a treatment of the specifics of the constitution in Locke's day.

21 *Republica*, I, chap. 16, p. 65.

22 *Republica*, I, chap. 20, p. 72.

23 *Republica*, I, chap. 22, p. 73.

24 *Republica*, I, chap 23, p. 74; II, chap. 2, p. 79.

25 *Republica*, I, chap. 24, p. 76.

26 *Republica*, I, chap. 18, p. 68.

27 *Republica*, I, chap. 18, p. 68.

28 *Republica*, I, chap. 24, p. 77; II, chap. 2, p. 79.

29 *Republica*, I, chap. 24, p. 76.

30 *Republica*, II, chap. 1, p. 79.

31 *Second Treatise*, §§37, 46, 47.

32 Tully, *Discourse on Property*, p. 147.

33 Ibid., p. 150; *Second Treatise*, §184.

34 Tully, *Discourse on Property*, pp. 149–51, 176.

35 Ibid., p. 176; *Education*, §110.

36 *Education*, §§103–5.

37 *Education*, §126; *Essay*, II, xxi, 34.

38 Tully, *Discourse on Property*, pp. 131–32, 137–38, for a discussion of Locke on charity.

39 This was certainly one of the guiding moral, social, and political principles of Cicero, whom Locke placed in the category of "truly great men," considering *On Duties* the surest guide in ethics after the New Testament. See *Works*, vol. 3, p. 483; *Education*, §185; Locke to Edward Clarke, 29 January/8 February [1686], *Correspon-*

dence, no. 844; "Draft Letter to the Countess of Peterborough, 1697," in *Education*, p. 395; "Some Thoughts Concerning Reading and Study for a Gentleman," in *Education*, p. 400. Since Cicero can be called the founder of the natural law tradition, it is perplexing that Tully never discusses him in reference to Locke. Had Tully paid some attention to Cicero, he might have a clearer understanding of Locke's moral and social values.

40 *Poor Laws*.

41 *Poor Laws*, pp. 382–83.

42 Tully, *Discourse on Property*, especially pp. 133–35, for Locke's views on the family.

43 Ibid., pp. 133–34.

44 Ibid., pp. 134, 143, 146, 169.

45 The following discussion of Locke and patriarchalism is indebted to the valuable study of Gordon Schochet, *Patriarchalism in Political Thought: The Authoritarian Family and Political Speculation and Attitudes Especially in Seventeenth-Century England* (New York: Basic Books, 1975), especially chap. 13. Keith Tribe, on whom Tully relies for a number of points (*Discourse on Property*, pp. 134, 136, 140, 143, 149, 169, 179), would evidently reject the latter's interpretation of Locke on the family. See Tribe, *Land, Labour and Economic Discourse* (London: Routledge and Kegan Paul, 1978), p. 51, where he says that the kind of discourse to which Hobbes's *Leviathan* and the *Two Treatises* belong "turns obstinately on a patriarchal form of organisation that had been the currency of 'civil society' since the time of Plato."

46 *Second Treatise*, §82.

47 *Second Treatise*, §72.

48 *Second Treatise*, §116.

49 *First Treatise*, §§37, 91; also §§92–98, 111.

50 Tully, *Discourse on Property*, pp. 133–34.

51 For example, *Second Treatise*, §§38, 45, 117, 120.

52 Tully, *Discourse on Property*, pp. 164–65.

53 Ibid., p. 165.

54 *Second Treatise*, §120.

55 Tully, *Discourse on Property*, pp. 153–54.

56 Ibid., p. 154.

57 Ibid., pp. 148–49.

58 C. B. Macpherson, *The Political Theory of Possessive Individualism: Hobbes to Locke* (Oxford: Clarendon Press, 1962), p. 212.

59 Ibid., p. 173. The citations are to *Second Treatise*, §§5, 158; John Dunn, *The Political Thought of John Locke: An Historical Account of the Argument of the "Two Treatises of Government"* (Cambridge: Cambridge University Press, 1969); and J. H. Plumb, *The Growth of Political Stability in England, 1675–1725* (London: Penguin, 1967).

60 *Second Treatise*, §§157, 158.

61 For the discussion that follows see in particular, in addition to Dunn and Plumb, Derek Hirst, *The Representative of the People? Voters and Voting in England Under the Early Stuarts* (Cambridge: Cambridge University Press, 1975), chaps. 1–3, 5, 7, 10; David Ogg, *England in the Reign of Charles II*, 2nd ed. (1956; rpt. in one volume, London and Oxford: Oxford University Press, 1967), pp. 472–83.

62 Tully, *Discourse on Property*, pp. 104–18, and especially 135–45.

63 Ibid., p. 106. See *Essay*, II, xxvii, 26.

64 Ibid., p. 138.

65 *Second Treatise*, §28. The "Turfs" perhaps mean peat.

66 *Second Treatise*, §§23, 24, 85, 172.

67 *First Treatise*, §130.

68 My general treatment of labor in this paragraph relies on Ann Kussmaul, *Servants in Husbandry in Early Modern England* (Cambridge: Cambridge University Press, 1981), chap. 1; K. I. Vaughan, *John Locke: Economist and Social Scientist* (Chicago: University of Chicago Press, 1980), pp. 83 ff.

69 For a discussion of the various kinds of seventeenth-century English agrarian laborers, see chap. 3 of the present volume.

70 Vaughan, *Locke*, p. 83.

71 *Second Treatise*, ∮85; also ∮86.

72 Tully, *Discourse on Property*, p. 137.

73 *First Treatise*, ∮42.

74 Tully, *Discourse on Property*, p. 137.

75 *First Treatise*, ∮43.

76 Tully, *Discourse on Property*, p. 142.

77 Ibid., pp. 140–41.

78 Harry Braverman, *Labor and Monopoly Capital: The Degradation of Work in the Twentieth Century*, foreword by Paul M. Sweezy (New York and London: Monthly Review Press, 1974), pp. 70–72.

79 Ibid., p. 70.

80 Ibid., p. 59.

81 Ibid., p. 61.

82 Marx, *Capital*, vol. 1 (Moscow: Progress Publishers, n.d.), pp. 477–78.

83 See Ellen Meiksins Wood, "The Separation of the Economic and the Political in Capitalism," *New Left Review*, 127 (May-June 1981), pp. 66–95.

CHAPTER SIX

1 Fulton H. Anderson, *The Philosophy of Francis Bacon* (Chicago: University of Chicago Press, 1948), pp. 299, 302; Anderson, *Francis Bacon: His Career and His Thought* (Los Angeles: University of Southern California Press, 1962), pp. 11, 334; John W. Yolton, *John Locke and the Way of Ideas* (Oxford: Clarendon Press, 1956),

p. 78; Yolton, *Locke and the Compass of Human Understanding* (Cambridge: Cambridge University Press, 1970), pp. 1, 7, 44, 55, 62, 76–77, 201.

2 See my article, "The Baconian Character of Locke's *Essay*," *Studies in History and Philosophy of Science*, 6 (1975), pp. 43–84; and my book, *The Politics of Locke's Philosophy: A Social Study of "An Essay Concerning Human Understanding"* (Berkeley and Los Angeles: University of California Press, 1983), chaps. 4–6.

3 See chaps. 3–4 of the present volume.

4 I have long been indebted for this insight to Professor M. M. Goldsmith of the University of Exeter.

5 *Second Treatise*, ⸹⸹87, 212, 227, 242.

6 *Second Treatise*, ⸹3.

7 *Second Treatise*, ⸹37. See chap. 4 of the present volume.

8 Much of what follows on the *Essay* in the remainder of this chapter, unless otherwise indicated, is derived from my book, *The Politics of Locke's Philosophy*.

9 Locke, *Conduct*, p. 39.

10 Edward Waterhouse, *The Gentlemans Monitor; or, A Sober Inspection into the Virtue, Vices, and Ordinary Means of the Rise and Decay of Men and Families* (1665), quoted in Lawrence Stone, ed., *Social Change and Revolution in England, 1540–1640* (London: Longmans, 1965), p. 136.

11 Quoted in Rowland Edmund Prothero, Baron Ernle, *English Farming, Past and Present*, introductions by G. E. Fussell and O. R. McGregor, 6th ed. (London: Heinemann and Frank Cass, 1961), p. 86.

12 Ibid., p. 105.

13 *Sylva*, "To The Reader."

14 Ibid., p. 120.

15 Ibid., p. 132.

16 Ibid.

17 For example, see Locke's remarks in *1692*, cited in chap. 3 in the present volume; and also the reference to the views of Nehemiah Grew.

18 *Essay*, III, x–xi; IV, xv–xvi.

19 *Essay*, IV, xvi, 4; xix, 2; xx, 4.

20 *Essay*, IV, xx, 6.

21 James L. Axtell, "Introduction," in *The Educational Writings of John Locke* (Cambridge: Cambridge University Press, 1968), p. 51.

22 *Education*, "Epistle Dedicatory," p. 111.

23 *Education*, ∮216.

24 *Education*, "Epistle Dedicatory," p. 112.

25 *Education*, "Epistle Dedicatory," pp. 112–13.

26 *Education*, ∮193.

27 *Education*, ∮195.

28 *Education*, ∮∮201–9.

29 *Education*, ∮204.

30 *Education*, ∮205.

31 *Education*, ∮206.

32 *Sylva*, "To the Reader."

33 *Sylva*, "To the Reader."

34 *Sylva*, "To the Reader."

35 *Sylva*, "To the King."

36 *Sylva*, p. 4.

37 *Education*, ∮210. Also see ∮211.

38 *Poor Laws*.

39 Locke to Clarke, 25 February 1698, *Correspondence*, no. 2398.

40 Ibid.

CHAPTER SEVEN

1 On Hobbes as more of a "French political thinker," see the provocative comments in Jonathan M. Wiener, "Quentin Skinner's Hobbes," *Political Theory*, 2 (August 1974), p. 256; and in Ellen Meiksins Wood, "The State and Popular Sovereignty in French Political Thought: A Genealogy of Rousseau's 'General Will,'" *History of Political Thought*, 4 (Summer 1983), pp. 281–315. Of course, Hobbes should not be dismissed for failing to perceive and analyze some of the fundamental problems of English society and polity. On this point, see my "Thomas Hobbes and the Crisis of the English Aristocracy," *History of Political Thought*, I (Autumn 1980), pp. 437–52. Also on Locke and Hobbes, see my book, *The Politics of Locke's Philosophy: A Social Study of "An Essay Concerning Human Understanding"* (Berkeley and Los Angeles: University of California Press, 1983), chap. 8.

2 Barbara J. Shapiro, *Probability and Certainty in Seventeenth-Century England: A Study of the Relationships Between Natural Science, Religion, History, Law, and Literature* (Princeton: Princeton University Press, 1983), p. 14.

3 See James Moore, "Locke and the Scottish Jurists," a paper presented to a conference on John Locke and the political thought of the 1680s sponsored by the Conference for the Study of Political Thought, Folger Shakespeare Library, Washington, D.C., March 21–23, 1980, pp. 30–31.

Index

153

Designer: Barbara Llewellyn
Compositor: Interactive Composition Corp.
Printer: Braun-Brumfield, Inc.
Binder: Braun-Brumfield, Inc.
Text: Plantin
Display: Plantin